CONVERSATIONS *with* CAGNEY

The Early Years

By BILL ANGELOS

WITH CONTRIBUTIONS FROM:
Dayna DeCarlo
Lisa Sanita
Stone Wallace

Conversations with Cagney: The Early Years
© 2019. Bill Angelos. All rights reserved.

All illustrations are copyright of their respective owners, and are also reproduced here in the spirit of publicity. Whilst we have made every effort to acknowledge specific credits whenever possible, we apologize for any omissions, and will undertake every effort to make any appropriate changes in future editions of this book if necessary.

No part of this book may be reproduced in any form or by any means, electronic, mechanical, digital, photocopying or recording, except for the inclusion in a review, without permission in writing from the publisher.

Published in the USA by:
BearManor Media
P O Box 71426
Albany, Georgia 31708
www.bearmanormedia.com

Printed in the United States of America

ISBN   978-1-62933-410-3 (paperback)
           978-1-62933-411-0 (hardcover)

Book design and layout by Darlene Swanson • www.van-garde.com

Contents

	How I Met James Cagney	1
Chapter 1	Once A Song-and-Dance-Man...	5
Chapter 2	Heading Home	13
Chapter 3	Yorkville Tar	17
Chapter 4	The Peabody	25
Chapter 5	Nut Club Baseball	33
Chapter 6	James Sr.	43
Chapter 7	Settlement House	51
Chapter 8	Show Business	59
Chapter 9	Stage Fright	66
Chapter 10	Panic Island	75
Chapter 11	Broadway	83
Chapter 12	The Palace	99
Chapter 13	Dance School	105
Chapter 14	Invade the Theater	119
Chapter 15	Presence	125
Chapter 16	Flash Acts	129
Chapter 17	The Tonys	139
Chapter 18	Fresh Mutt	143
Chapter 19	Zanuck	155
Chapter 20	SAG	163

Chapter 21	Real Gangsters................177
Chapter 22	New York Bound..............185
Chapter 23	Just A Job...................211
Chapter 24	Hollywood...................221
Chapter 25	Awareness...................247
Chapter 26	Still Tough..................251
Chapter 27	The Faraway Fella.............257
	Epilogue....................259
	Reflections from the Contributors...263
	Acknowledgements.............269

How I Met James Cagney

LOOKING BACK ALL THOSE years…. The entire experience feels almost dreamlike. The pages that follow are proof indeed that this was no dream, but one of the most memorable and deeply felt experiences of my life.

From the moment I first entered the room and found myself in his presence, I immediately sensed that this was no ordinary man. In fact, this was no ordinary movie star. As a writer in Hollywood, I'd met and worked with many of the giants in film and television. But this man was somehow different. He seemed to exude a powerful aura that filled the entire room. And yet… and yet… there was also a kind of warmth and gentleness in his presence that invited you in closer.

Standing next to me was the man responsible for it all — actor Martin Sheen. He'd driven me up to Verney Farm, as Mr. Cagney's home was known back then. Martin was in the middle of rehearsal for a TV drama in which he played President John F. Kennedy and I can remember him practicing his Kennedy voice as we drove upstate.

A few weeks before that, Sheen had been at an event that Mr. Cagney had also attended. The two had never met before, but Mr. Cagney called him over to speak with him.

"Can you dance, kid?" he said to a somewhat surprised Martin, who couldn't dance a lick.

But in the conversation that followed, Cagney asked Sheen if he would be interested in making a biographical film in which he (Sheen) would play Cagney.

Sheen of course was thrilled at the opportunity presented to him – My God, the prospect of portraying one of the greatest screen legends ever! – and told Cagney he felt honored by The Man himself to have been chosen to do so, and almost immediately set out to find someone to write the screenplay.

Sheen had just participated in a major one-night only stage event that I had written and co-produced at Kennedy Center for the Performing Arts in Washington D.C. called "Night of the First Americans". It featured more than a dozen famous stars, and more than 150 representatives from more than 40 Native American Tribal entitles.

Evidentially Sheen liked the way I'd handled that endeavor, so one day he and his then- business partner Bill Greenblatt dropped by my home in Malibu and asked if I'd be interested in taking a shot at the screenplay. Well, of course I was, and a day or so later we met with Marge Zimmerman (head of all things Cagney, fact be known) who would be doing the final picking. That too went well. In fact, it was Marge who suggested I come up to Mr. Cagney's home in upstate New York and stay a while.

When I got there they graciously gave me a little house on the property to stay in, and also the loan of a car. One day while driving around the area I happened on a little roadside stand and went inside to look around. There on the counter was something I hadn't seen in years; one of those old video disc-playing machines. Next to it was a box of movies on discs, that contained five Cagney films, including his first starring role– the classic 1931 gangster drama *The Public Enemy*. So once or twice a week Mr. Cagney and I sat back and watched each of those films together. That is, I watched and was captivated by these wonderful pictures – while he watched and cried. He admitted that he'd never seen any of his films before.

Sad to say, although I taped all of my encounters with Mr. Cagney and the others, the tapes were lost in a fire. What follows are the remaining transcripts of what is now remembered as almost dreamlike.

One final remembrance. The night Martin came to pick me up, ending my five weeks in one of the most unusual and tightest relationships I would ever have in my life, we said our goodbyes, I got in the car with Martin, and immediately started to cry… and cry… and cry…

Dreamlike indeed…but an actuality I now share with you.

I hope you enjoy reading these memories as much as I enjoyed living them.

– Bill Angelos

Receiving the key from Mayor Koch with Bill

CHAPTER 1

Once A Song-and-Dance-Man...

A*LTHOUGH* J*AMES* C*AGNEY WON* an Academy Award for his performance as a song-and-dance-man in Yankee Doodle Dandy, few people remember him as such. A "Cagney movie" conjures up images of the tough guy gangster films of the '30's. And in truth, it was these films that catapulted Cagney into becoming, as the cliche goes, a legend in his own time.

In the '30's while America was experiencing the first serious crack in the Utopian facade promulgated by the Industrial Revolution, a new kind of hero-image began to emerge to fill the people's needs. The image of the guy who was willing, not only to fight 'The System' but to go down swinging. On the movie screen, no one personified this image with more electricity and excitement then James Cagney. And, he added his own touch . . . a smile.

Cagney was well aware of what it was like to be on the short end of The System, having been brought up in the streets of New York during the early part of the 20th century. Certainly his countless experiences as a cocky child-of-the-times contributed greatly to his ability to delineate this new hero image.

But this image, like of the screen personas he indelibly painted in our minds, were actually more the result of Cagney's supreme mastery that enabled him to perceive the rhythm and movements of the Song and Dance of Life and manifest them on the screen with the same seemingly effortless ease inherent in the Picasso life study.

Cagney, like Picasso, was an innovator, a filmic innovator. Cagney's life story will also bring something else into focus that we believe is alarmingly relevant in today's world. That 'something' while always very much a part of his on-screen portrayals, was also fundamental in Cagney's offscreen life. It's the same 'something' that lies at the heart of this country's greatness... the same 'something' that threatens to be undermined by Society's present thrust. The importance of the individual.

Cagney was literally a man of the 20th century. And as such, his life and the roles he played reflect the changes that this country has undergone during and even beyond his lifetime.

His reply: "Nothing strange about it."

The streets were not the crowded teaming kind we associate with the Lower East Side. They are remembered as comparatively empty. A Sunday morning, the time when people usually went walking. The settings are clearly remembered by him and should perhaps be a means of getting into specific scenic environments.

NOTE: In fact, it was Cagney's extraordinary powers of recollection that gave me the insight which led a novel approach to writing the screenplay. In stark contrast to his mental acuity, I was somewhat taken aback by the toll diabetes had taken on his physical presence. Moreover, his frequent bouts with the accompanying pain underscored the reality of the situation. It only took two or three days of beginning our morning sessions eating breakfast together on the deck of the main house for me to announce my revelation: Cagney would appear as himself in the movie about himself. Of course he understood immediately what I was implying. He'd have to stay alive for the project to be completed.

Cagney and his wife agreed to come to New York with us and point out some of the more important locations and to meet the cast. Certainly, the studios want us to go easy on Warner and Zanuck and their participation. The Cagney family want us to go easy on the family image, Mom and Dad.

First begin with stills and then let the stills come to life and we would be in that period. We'd use Mayor Koch.

James Cagney: He'd hate it.

Bill Angelos: Would he? Places in New York. They just did a piece on *The Today Show* and it's similar to what I was going to talk to Mr. C about.

BA: Seeing the places as they are today and remembering them as they were then. And dissolving back to that period. Only instead of this Mayor, we'd use Mayor Koch.

Marge Zimmerman: Mayor Koch gave him that. He never gave a gift to anybody but Jim. That's true. Pat (O'Brien) will tell you that. He gave that to Jimmy *(The Key to New York)*. He adores Jamsie. Why does he adore you? He doesn't know you.

JC: That's right.

MZ: He does, though, he really loves Jamsie.

Mayor Koch

BA: You see what's going to happen in the film, we will begin real small and we're going to do a film. Not too many people know about it. But then, as the word gets out, things start to build especially like when we go into New York. They hear we're going to be doing some of the filming there, all of a sudden, Mayor Koch comes out. We hear from William Fugazy *(Fugazy International)* and the Yankees, and it starts to build, you see.

JC: FUCK!!!

BA: Whooah!

JC: I didn't say that *(laughter)*.

BA: So that will be the frame of the canvas.

JC: And that's the way it's gonna happen.

BA: So, going back to this thing I mentioned to you. It gives us a form where we can say and do a lot of different things. We can comment on today's scene.

JC: I don't have to keep in perspective.

BA: No. We can move back and forth whenever we want to.

JC: Yeah.

BA: But understand, you now become the glue of the film, you and Martin will be in the film and he will be playing you early on, but you, now become what holds the film together. It could be a real, unusual and unique film.

JC: Sounds good.

BA: So what we'll do for these next couple of weeks when I'm here is it shouldn't be a strain because the important thing is for you to get ready for the film, to get better. It is to start painting the pictures of the past. The early years, the vaudeville years which were obviously an important part of the foundation, right? And then the movie years. The formation of the Screen Actors Guild, *The Public Enemy* and the years after. As far as the body of the film is concerned. And maybe as we invite other people in for example, Jack Lemmon. You and Lemmon might do a turn that takes us into *Mister Roberts* period.

BA: Do you and Pat O'Brien talk to each other about those days before you knew each other?

Jim & Pat: pals for a lifetime in *Ragtime*

JC: Oh yeah. He's a good guy to remember. He has a perfect recollection of every instant.

BA: I thought that maybe a conversation with the two of you would set up those early sequences for us. Did he grow up in the same area?

JC: Oh no. He was from Milwaukee.

BA: You and Pat O'Brien might do a thing that takes us into another scene, so that we bring the real people in.

JC: As they appear.

BA: Exactly. And then we would have others playing them in the earlier years. But all the time beginning with the reality wherever possible, and then moving back.

Jim & Jim Sr.

CHAPTER 2

Heading Home

Martin Sheen playing Cagney: He's supposed to be a tough guy. Yes, there's a softness.

The question of Martin's dancing.

JC: The essential comes up regardless of where the hell you are. What the person is, comes through.

JC: You're not discouraged, are you?

Martin: Of course I am.

JC: Good. You're off the picture. *They look at each other and chuckle.*

Sign: *Taconic State Parkway*

Martin: Taconic, I guess that's an Indian name.

JC: Our version of it.

Aerial shot of the Limo

Harvey driving the Limo. He is a strongly good-looking man in his early '50's. He sits behind the wheel of the limo with a certain elan that tells us he is doing exactly what he wants to be doing. Behind him, we can see Martin and Cagney looking out of their respective windows as the limo comes off the Third Avenue Bridge and winds its way down East River Drive. Cagney's attention suddenly turns to Harvey.

JC: Harvey, what do you say we show Martin the old neighborhood?

Harvey: Sure thing Mr. C.

JC: If you're gonna play me, you might as well see where it all began for me.

Exit 86th St Limo turning off.

JC: I'll bet I've been asked a thousand times what it was like growing up on New York's Lower East Side.

Martin: I'll make it a thousand and one.

JC: That's the point. I didn't grow up on the New York's Lower East Side.

Martin: You didn't?

At the corner of 79th St and First Avenue.

JC: 79th St. and 1st Avenue. This was the center of my universe.

Martin: And it wasn't at all like the Lower East Side?

We see Apartment Building and the accoutrements of the 1980's.

JC: You mean the streets teaming with immigrants speaking a hundred different languages and outdoor vendors huckstering their wares in at least fifty of them?

Martin (*laughing*): Well yes.

JC: I'm afraid not.

Martin: I don't imagine it looked much like this either.

Cagney staring out the window.

JC: God how it's changed. The buildings. The people. The sounds.

Cagney reaches over and pushes the button that rolls down his window.

Martin: The sounds?

Bus tire screeching, car horn. Two kids walking down the street to the rocking music emanating from their portable ghetto blaster.

Cagney reacting to the raucous sounds of today's 79th St.

Martin: You mean the sounds were different then?

The look on Cagney's face begins to soften.

JC: There was an organ. I remember an organ.

The sound of the organ becomes dominant and the scene outside his window freezes and is transformed into 79th St. circa 1910.

JC: And there were all those kids that danced in the streets. The lovely face of a 12-year-old blonde girl. Georgiana, a blonde girl. Czech girl, she'd follow the organ sound. The equally lovely face of a 10-year-old brunette girl. She and Lily Flower used to dance to the organ. They were good too.

At fourteen, a tried and true member of the gang known as "The Up-The-Blocks," Jim took time out from his many activities for this informal shot.

CHAPTER 3

Yorkville Tar

JC: Where to begin? The contradictions that one lives with over on the East Side. The pretty girls, Marie Cody, beautiful girl. She was a sister of Joe Cody and Bill Cody, neither of them could fight worth a lick. And that was your gauge. Bill Cody's path crossed mine when there was a knock on the front door of the flat we had and the kid said, "Hey Jim, Joe Cody has a fight with Ken. He's fighting now." So I say okay and I put the cap on and when I got down there Cody was on the ground. He was a tough kid and I said, "Take it easy, I'll take your place Joe." He couldn't breathe. He was hit in the kidneys, in the back, and you know what that can do to ya. He stayed down and when he got up, Kenny, and it never occurred to me he was little, I was little. So when we started again I feinted and flew one and hit him on the chin, all he did was this (*hardly a flinch*). Very discouraging…Bang! He didn't go down. Hit 'em right on the (*gestures to the chin*). Great little guy.

BA: Where would you say, what has changed then between now and then?

School days at PS 158

JC: Different, different kind of people. Different kind.

BA: But do you think we're motivated by the same anxieties and emotions as people were then?

JC: To a lesser degree now. You use to be able to get an armful of vegetables for nothing. Couldn't do it now.

BA: Were you having fun?

Harry, Bill, & Jim

JC: It was the need of the moment. The need of the moment. I had an older brother, Harry. Muscles in his ears. Powerful. At thirteen or fourteen everything stood out like a strong man. And couldn't fight worth a goddamn. Whenever he got in a jam, he'd say to the other fella, "I got a brother that can lick you."

BA: So it was always you they turned to.

JC: Imagine! You see he couldn't fight worth a damn.

JC: So much pops up in the mind. This chap and I, we stole potatoes, built a fire and Theodore's brother and I went down to the empty lot and we heated the potatoes, ate 'em camping out.

BA: Camping out in NY.

JC: And there was nothing exciting about it particularly.

BA: Was that in the old neighborhood?

JC: Yeah 79th St.

BA: So, if we went to 79th St. there used to be an empty lot. Today the chances are there's not an empty lot there anymore. No, nothing.

BA: Other images?

JC: There was a kosher chicken market down on 79th St. and 1st. When they brought the chickens in, we were thrown out.

BA: You couldn't buy anything there, either?

JC: No (*laughter*). You hear that all day long.

BA: Cackling, they're talking about chickens.

JC: Wonderful. The day they went down by the fire, I went looking for them, the two brothers, Sparrow and . . . I can't think of the other one. And that's almost 70 years ago, more than 70 years ago. Yet clear as a bell.

BA: Did you say there was a fire going on?

JC: There was a fire when the chicken market burned down. We didn't do it.

BA: You say you went looking for the Coughlin brothers?

JC: But they were no longer there. Two nice kids. They were about 14, 15.

BA: Were they blamed?

JC: Oh no.

BA: Do you think the fire was set maliciously?

JC: No. It was quite a conflagration.

BA: Really? Was it implied that was the case?

JC: I don't know. It was too long ago. It was a comfortable time.

BA: Can you elaborate on that word when you say a 'comfortable' time?

JC: No one wanted anything of anybody. We stole potatoes off the stands, nobody missed them.

Lenox Hill Gang

On the previous day we had been at a Sports Luncheon in New York City. Rod Carew in receiving an award said this about his hitting ability: "Some people think hitting is hard. But for me it's easy."

In drawing a parallel to Carew's ability to hit a ball and Cagney's fighting prowess.

JC: We just did what was natural. Didn't ask any questions about it. We just did it. My first fight? Mickey McKenernie. I was running down the street. I was ten years old. We had just moved into the neighborhood. So the big guys put Mickey McKenernie on me to see what I was made of. They shouldn't have done that. So I was runnin' down, and he came out and took a slug at me and I proceeded to polish him off. And my kid brother, four years old, didn't want to see me get in trouble and he hit Mickey. And I remember my father behind the bar. Apron on. And…I was outside fighting. His saloon was on the corner of 79th Street and First Avenue. And here is his boy, Jimmy. Everything flying. And my old man heard the commotion…went outside and saw me…looked and went back inside. And while I was fighting Kenny, a little Jewish woman said, "Somebody send for the police! These boys are killing each other." We were having fun. My mother was standing alongside of this woman and she said, "Let 'em alone."

BA: What about fear in those days?

JC: Oh, it was there. I remember once running down 96th St. at dusk and suddenly one of those things, you know what they used to raise the wagons with? Pulley. It came off the roof and hit my heel. Somebody saw me running and threw this thing at me. If it had hit me it would have killed me. Then my grandfather appeared. "Jamsie, your mother wants you." Here's this tough kid and his mother wants him. And I got up in the hallway and my brother Harry says, "Hey Red." I was the only one in the family that they called Red. I was pronouncedly Red, and I said "What?" He says, "They're gonna stick a big needle up yer ass!" I said, "Like hell they are!" And I cut for the street. And he came down and he grabbed me, and my grandfather too and we go back up. My youngest brother Bill had diphtheria and they wanted to give me an inoculation and I didn't want it. So they took my pants down and the doctor put some cold water on a napkin or something and put it on me and he says, "That isn't bad is it?" I said, "No, that's okay." Bang! And he hit me with it.

BA: His dad seeing you fighting, would Jamsie have wanted him to stop it?

JC: Oh no.

BA: He did the right thing.

JC: Oh sure, he was minding his own business. And he was a fighter, too, of sorts.

BA: Then you were pretty much on your own in that environment. You were taking care of business.

JC: As it happened.

BA: So that's where it began. Where it begins for us all. Where you pick up how you approach life and dealt with it as it happened.

JC: Until somebody came along.

BA: What happened to the fighting? Was it there? Was there no need for it?

JC: No. I got a job at the Lenox Hill. I was kind of a cop. I kept the bums out of the club. It was a typical settlement house club. They put me on the door and when people came with their admission things I would take them, put them in a box. I was feeling very low one night. What I was low about I don't know. And this kid says, "Jim they've broken in downstairs (the prop room)," so I dashed down and started punching. And three or four boys from the Dramatic Club, one big strong guy and he followed me. We punched our way through those mugs. One of the guys that John was chasing turned and saw that he was 6'2" and he says, "You're too big for me, what do I wanna fight you for?! And John banged him so after that all the blueness had gone, I worked it off. From that point on we went on just the same. It was amazing to me that at no time did anyone pull a 'jack' and belt us with it. These were tough kids.

CHAPTER 4

The Peabody

BA: But there was somebody who taught you how to do a specific dance, the Peabody?

JC: Yes, it was a social dance.

BA: Which was a patterned dance and in what setting would you dance it.

JC: Dance hall. A friend of mine was a good dancer and he showed me the Peabody.

BA: And the girls were part of your life by then.

JC: Yes, I looked over to Joey and he was the one who taught me to dance. And was nodding.

BA: Did you go over and ask someone to dance?

JC: Oh sure. The music was Victrola at the time.

BA: Any particular song come to mind?

WWI Draft Card

JC: *I'll Be Down to Get You in A Taxi Honey.*

BA: So you liked the ladies and dance was a way of communicating.

WWI Draft Card

JC: Oh sure. I was fifteen when I met Nellie. She was a great dancer, much better then I of course. And she knew the Peabody. And we danced and we became sweethearts.

BA: What did that entail in those days?

The S. A. T. C.

A general outline of the purpose of the S. A. T. C. is contained in a letter from the War Department addressed to all the colleges of the United States late in August, as follows:

1. All young men, who were planning to go to school this fall, should carry out their plans and do so. Each should go to the college of his choice, matriculate and enter as a regular student. He will, of course, also register with his local board on the registration day set by the President. As soon as possible after registration day, probably on or about October first, opportunity will be given for all the regularly-enrolled students to be inducted into the Students' Army Training Corps at the schools where they are in attendance. Thus the Corps will be organized by voluntary induction under the Selective Service Act, instead of by enlistment as previously contemplated.

The student, by voluntary induction, becomes a soldier in the United States Army, uniformed, subject to military discipline and with the pay of a private. He will simultaneously be placed on full active duty and contracts will be made as soon as possible, with the colleges for the housing, subsistence and instruction of the student soldiers.

2. Officers, uniforms, rifles and such other equipment as may be available will be furnished by the War Department.

3. The student-soldiers will be given military instruction under officers of the Army and will be kept under observation and test to determine their qualification as officer-candidates, and technical experts such as engineers, chemists and doctors. After a certain period, the men will be selected according to their performance, and assigned to military duty in one of the following ways:

(a) He may be transferred to a central officers' training camp.
(b) He may be transferred to a non-commissioned officers' training school.
(c) He may be assigned to the school where he is enrolled for further intensive work in a specified line for a limited specified time.
(d) He may be assigned to the vocational training section of the Corps for technical training of military value.
(e) He may be transferred to a cantonment for duty with troops as a private.

4. Similar sorting and reassignment of the men will be made at periodical intervals, as the requirements of the service demand. It can not now be definitely stated how long a particular student will remain at college. This will depend on the requirements of the mobilization and age group to which he belongs. In order to keep the unit at adequate strength, men will be admitted from secondary schools or transferred from Depot Brigades as the need may require.

5. No units of the Students' Army Training Corps will, for the present, be established at secondary schools, but it is hoped to provide at an early date for the extension of military instruction in such schools.

6. There will be both a collegiate section and a vocational section of the Students' Army Training Corps. Young men of draft age of grammar school education, will be given opportunity to enter the vocational section of the Corps.

7. In view of the comparatively short time during which most of the student-soldiers will remain in college and the exacting military duties awaiting them, academic instruction must necessarily be modified along lines of direct military value. The War Department will prescribe or suggest such modifications. The schedule of purely military instruction will not preclude effective academic work. It will vary to some extent in accordance with the type of academic instruction, e. g., will be less in a medical school than in a college of liberal arts.

8. The primary purpose of the Students' Army Training Corps is to utilize the executive and teaching personel and the physical equipment of the colleges to assist in the training of our new armies. This imposes great responsibilities on the colleges and at the same time creates an exceptional opportunity for service. The colleges are asked to devote the whole energy and educational power of the institution to the phases and lines of training desired by the Government. The problem is a new one and calls for inventiveness and adaptability as well as that spirit of cooperation which the colleges have already so abundantly shown.

—98—

The SATC

The Early Years

The first and the last formal formations of the S. A. T. C.

The SATC Commons

JC: Just talk.

BA: Would you kiss? Was kissing allowed?

JC: Oh sure. Oh, she was ON!

"Jimmy Cagney's a nice young man. He comes to the door with his hat in his hand......"

I've forgotten what the rest of it is.

BA: In 1916 there was a war going on.

JC: I was in the SATC (Student Army Training Corp) at Columbia University. Saturday Afternoon Tea Club. Remember that? We were studying to be Lieutenants. And for my girlfriend, I was a lieutenant as far as she was concerned. A 98-lb. bum. Didn't have any military sense at all. When Nellie introduced me to her father, she said, "Poppa I want you to meet Lieutenant Cagney."

Jim entered Columbia on February 1918 and left after the war ended in November 1918, a month after his father passed away. No longer funding his tuition and having to support his family full time he left Columbia.

JC: I went with Nellie until I went into show business. My brother Harry was a medical student and he was the one who prompted me to make an application to the SATC, and I did and they took me. Why I don't know. And when it was over it was over and I got my discharge.

World War I ended November 11, 1918.

BA: You got any feelings about that? Where you connected to it?

JC: A thing of the moment.

BA: Now the next step, granted, it's of the moment, but it's a transitional step, from that to show business.

JC: I didn't know what the hell was going on. Nothing. (*A born existentialist!*)

Remember the old chow line for the S. A. T. C. Commons?

Final Day

Yorkville Nut Club

Nut Club Baseball

CHAPTER 5

Nut Club Baseball

BA: You were playing ball early on too. What position did you play?

JC: Catcher.

BA: Were you serious about it?

JC: Oh yeah. I was going to the big leagues. It was a cinch.

BA: And you played ball into your 20's.

JC: Yeah sure.

BA: Was there any conflict between that and the acting?

JC: When something happened or where I couldn't play, I would lay off the acting and play ball.

BA: There's that wonderful story about you going up to Sing Sing to play ball and there were all your old cronies there.

At bat

Stuyvesant High School

JC: I didn't know any of them. But they all knew me. "Hello Red do you go down to the East Side park anymore?"

BA: So there was some kind of quality that was working even then.

JC: I suppose.

BA: You know there are societies that believe if you're left-handed, it's not good, right?

Mike Donlin

JC: Funny in the head.

BA: Even the word 'sinister' comes from that, it means left.

JC: You know that they use to call left handers 'cockeyes.'

BA: No, is that right?

JC: Yeah, when I was a kid, Mike Donlin was left handed of the New York Giants. But he was a hell of a hitter.

Donlin played for the NY Giants from 7/19/99 - 10/1/14, with a .333 batting average.

BA: Were you a fan of a particular team in the early days?

How do you like Lee Tracy, George Raft and Jim Cagney in baseball regalia—participants in the Comedians vs. Leading Men Charity Baseball Game at Wrigley Field.

With Lee Tracy & George Raft at a Celebrity game, 1935

JC: Oh, the Giants. Oh sure.

BA: They were playing in the Polo Ground in those days, did it exist then?

JC: Yeah, on 155th and 157th Streets.

BA: So you use to go with the kids and the games.

JC: My father used to take us.

BA: And you got the bug and wanted to play.

JC: Oh yeah.

BA: Was there a team early on in the neighborhood?

JC: I played for the Yorkville Nut Club.

BA: Was it the same club then that eventually went up to Sing Sing?

JC: Yeah, we got an invitation to play up there from the Mutual Welfare League. They beat the tar out of us.

BA: So you guys stayed together for a while.

JC: Oh yes. Neilly Finn played short stop. Roy Cleaver a Jewish guy, hell of a third baseman. He behaved like a madman.

BA: In what way?

JC: Behave on the field.

BA: Oh really?

JC: Brother O'Meara was second baseman, George Mitchell was first baseman, a Jewish boy played the outfield, can't think of his name, a hell of a runner. The fastest on the team. Peter ("Bootah") Hessling played outfield. Loggerhead Quinlavin was the second pitcher.

BA: (*laughter*) You can't be making up these names. You've got to have been there, terrific.

JC: Big, big head.

BA: Were there ever any scraps in the ball games?

JC: Sure. I'll never forget there was a guy up at bat and he said something, and I said something and he said something and I said something and before I knew it, the outfield was on its way in. They sensed it.

BA: Were the teams neighborhood teams. Was the Nut Club from around the 79th Street area?

JC: 81st St. was the John Jay's.

BA: Did you have your own lot, they didn't have school yards in those days?

JC: No.

BA: So you got a team together then you would play somebody from different areas.

JC: Corona. We would go to play them. Get beaten.

BA: So it was sort of an informal league?

JC: Yes.

BA: Were you in high school by then?

JC: I'm trying to think, high school. We played a team from Long Island and this was the team we fought with each other.

BA: You went to Stuyvesant. Did Nellie go to a Catholic girls' school?

JC: Yeah, generally where the girls went.

BA: I see that as a scene traveling out to Corona to play and a couple of the girls coming along or getting there perhaps a little late and you guys are suited up and all hell breaks loose.

JC: Oh sure. That's normal.

BA: What year was it when you played? How old were you when you played at Sing-Sing with the Nut Club?

JC: 1919.

BA: Did you still have aspirations of professional ball at the time? How close do you think you got?

JC: A scout for one of the 'B' teams, a gray-haired man, and he had me and Neilly Finn picked out for the Big Leagues.

BA: Did your dad ever come to the games?

JC: Sometimes he did. He and a chum.

BA: Was it a mixed emotion in seeing him when he could come to the game like that?

JC: I was happy to see him there. Didn't want to see him drunk.

Mr. & Mrs. James Cagney

CHAPTER 6

James Sr.

JC: W<small>E ALWAYS HAD</small> a piano in the house. My father, James Francis Cagney, was a drunk. He loved piano players and he'd pick 'em up and bring 'em home with him. My dad played the piano and learned by ear. I couldn't dance worth a damn. I could do comedy steps. One Thanksgiving I dressed up with old clothes, put a beard on and a derby hat, borrowed a coat my father had and I did this funny dance. I got laughs with it and that was enough. I always had elevation, why I don't know. My mother, Carolyn (Carrie) Cagney, had a nice alto and she used to sing. My father sang:

> I don't wanna play in your yard
> I don't like you any more
> You'll be sorry when you see me
> Sliding down my cellar door
>
> You can't holler down our rain barrel
> You can't climb our apple tree

> I don't wanna play in your yard
> If you can't be good to me.

And there were all those kids that danced in the streets.

BA: The music of the period, The Peabody and the song your dad sang.

JC: Oh, he was a lousy singer, drunk, drunk you know. He would get up in this saloon that was full of drunks and they'd say, "Shhh, the boy's gonna sing." And he'd sing:

> Oh, there's a pretty spot in Ireland. A spot that I call my land.
> (*with unbelievable vibrato from Cagney*) Boy was it sad.

BA: Did the two of you spend time together?

JC: No. I was his favorite son, too. He hardly knew me. I was Jim Junior. Dad looked like Gleason. He was a bum with every instinct of a bum. At seventeen he met my mother. He was introduced, "Jim I want you to meet Carolyn Nelson." And he turned around and there he was with a can of beer on his head. He was born here and my mother too.

BA: Did you ever talk to him about his drinking?

JC: Oh sure. There's a knock on the door, "Your father has a kid down there that he wants you to fight." My old man. So I said, "All right, I'll be right with you." So crossing the street, the Reception Hospital ambulance went at a hell of a clip up First Avenue. The old man made a gesture to the kid and fell in the tracks of the car drunk. We broke loose from him and got it on.

BA: When you say you talked to him about his drinking, did you ask him why or did you just tell him to please stop? What was your attitude toward him, was it pleading?

JC: We just sprung him from Blackwell's Island after doing six months.

BA: Oh boy.

JC: This was the thing. I said, "Do you want to go back to Blackwell's?" He looked at me and he never did.

BA: How long after that did he get ill, was it long after?

JC: A couple of years. He died on October 10, 1918.

In 1932 Blackwell Island Penitentiary was erected and named after its current owner Robert Blackwell. It was the first asylum in New York and was located in the NYC East River running from E 46th St. to 85th St., now known as Roosevelt Island.

The workhouse where Jim's dad spent six months was built in 1852 and it was for misdemeanor sentences, alcoholics and petty violators. It housed 1000 inmates required to perform some daily labor according to their skills.

BA: You understood him?

JC: After a fashion, yes. I couldn't understand why he drank so much. He'd come home on a Sunday morning loaded to the gills and sit down at the piano. He couldn't play worth a goddamn.

BA: Couldn't play and couldn't sing but that didn't stop him.

JC: Oh no he was 'ON.' He was a musician.

BA: Well it might be as simple as recently they've come to the realization that many people drink because it's an allergy, a chemical imbalance.

Blackwell Island Workhouse

JC: This could've been the story because he had popping eyes.

BA: And the strange thing about allergies is that when you're allergic to something you have a craving for it. Whether it's sugar or wheat or alcohol. You keep taking the substance not realizing that you're going the wrong way.

JC: And the thing with him was he was behind the bar. He drank on an average of 60 drinks a day.

BA: So he never knew in those days it weakened his condition and his organs?

JC: Oh sure. But it was an amazing recovery. He'd get drunk, fall off the piano stool, we'd put him to bed and when he'd wake up he was sick, sick as hell. Two weeks later he was eating steak for breakfast. My poor mother never drank a drop in her life.

BA: What was it between them on a day to day basis?

JC: Oh fine. She stayed with it. She had four boys. I'm amazed at what she put up with over the years.

JC: They were dropping like flies around here at the time.

BA: Do you remember when you found out and where you were?

JC: Well, I went in the army. Harry was, too; at the same time studying at Columbia. We got word that the ambulance had taken him off. Then Harry and I went over to Blackwell Island where he was dying and I got there at the hospital. I asked for James Cagney and by the expression on this woman's face I knew he had died. She said, "Oh no, he passed on earlier."

BA: They had taken him back to Blackwell's Island, which was for alcoholics? It was also a hospital.

JC: Yes.

BA: Is that an island off the East Side? How would you get there in those days?

JC: A tug back and forth.

BA: Then you had to go back and tell the family.

JC: Yes.

BA: It wasn't long after that you got out of the army.

JC: Oh yes, the war ended a month later November 11, 1918 and I was given an honorable discharge.

BA: Was it shortly after that you went and took a job on the stage?

JC: Same general period. Soon after came *Every Sailor*.

BA: So it was probably the next step once you were out. It really put an end to that period of your life with your dad's passing away. The next period would be when you went into . . .

JC: Show business.

BA: All the more reason then, sir, that's a major step.

JC: It's also a part of the game, part of the routine. Didn't know what the hell was going on but I did it just the same.

BA: Remember when your dad was really seriously ill? You did have an incident with a priest who said that he was going to come by.

JC: He never showed up. He took the money and never showed up.

BA: Did you feel any connection prior with the church or religion.

JC: Oh yeah. (*Jim was an altar boy*). My mother and father, too. They took a pledge: no more booze. Put the pledge in his pocket and went out and got drunk.

BA: In his last years he didn't have a saloon but he did have a saloon for a while. Were your mother and father the same age?

JC: Two years difference, he was older. Mom was born in 1877, Dad in 1875.

BA: When he met your mother and married her in 1897, the die was cast for him.

A young Carolyn (Carrie)

JC: He was already a boozer.

BA: He must have had something going for him, she fell for him.

JC: Oh yeah. I said to her one time, "Momma, why do you hang on to a guy like this?" God damn fool, the kind of person he is or was. She said, "Jimmy, he was nice."

BA: Was it diphtheria at the end, was that what undermined him eventually?

JC: Epidemic. Yeah flu.

BA: What quality about your mother remains uppermost in your mind?

JC: (*gestures*) Right straight down the middle. It was a helluva blow to her when I went into show business. But when I got the Oscar I went down and picked it up and I gave it to her. At the time she'd had a stroke and couldn't speak. I said, "It's all yours Mom."

BA: Why was it such a blow? Was it so alien to her?

JC: She figured I'd become an artist.

BA: The stage at that time was not considered upstanding.

JC: (*shaking his head*) Show business.

CHAPTER 7

Settlement House

BA: From ten, twelve, fourteen the artistic temperament started to show itself, didn't it?

JC: I would draw the funny papers when Dad brought home the paper.

BA: You're up there on a stage, did you have any feeling about going up there?

JC: There was a dramatic club in the Settlement, and I joined the group.

The Settlement House on East 76th St. offered kindergarten, lectures, plays, and a gym. There were classes for immigrants, coaching for civil service exams and where families can go with their troubles. In 1912 Mary Trenholm was the Head Worker and was daughter to President of the American Surety Company. She had the Bunny Hug and the Turkey Trot dances banned at the Settlement, claiming to the NY Times, "Subtle poison harming all our femininity".

76th St. Settlement House

BA: Were you interested in drama?

JC: They needed somebody to paint the scenery. So I was the one who painted it.

BA: So now you're working at the Settlement House, what kind of things did they do on stage?

JC: Classics. I wasn't the classic type, but they gave me a part. I read it and I could do it. That was the first ham thing that I attempted. Tommy Walsh said, "Jim would you do your part again?" I said, "For what?" He said, "I want the others to see how they should do it." So I did it again. This little tough guy that I was playing, and Tommy said to the others, "How do you like that?" And they applauded and of course this brought all the ham out.

BA: When you say this was the first 'ham' thing that you did . . .

JC: I did something that was good.

BA: Did it surprise you?

JC: Yeah! I thought I was just doing a normal thing.

BA: You say it was playing an aggressive character.

JC: I remember the lines. 'Don't pay any attention to him, lady. He doesn't know what he's talking about.' Then she answered me and I went on. Apparently it struck home.

BA: So now you were an actor. The phrase that strikes me as most important from what we've talked about so far, is your response to the moment. That notion of just watching what's going on and responding to it, moving with it, wherever it took you.

JC: That's right. The need of the moment. You did what needed to be done. I think that's what applied to the whole damn scheme of things.

BA: Was it a characteristic that was prevalent in other members of your family as well?

JC: No.

BA: Was it a sense of responsibility?

JC: I don't know. It was a thing to do.

BA: Was that instinct part of when you were doing movies? You could sense that on a set, too.

JC: A lot of it, yeah.

BA: What exactly was a Settlement House?

JC: People came with their troubles. My mother was there with one of the captive mothers in the area. Whenever there was a problem, she went to Miss Trenholm. There was a cop named Pat Galloway and he was making the rounds and a woman crossed his path one night and he tried to fuck her right then and there in the streets. The woman got to my mother and mother got to my father and my father got the charges dismissed from the woman falsely claimed by the cop. He did.

BA: Was Miss Trenholm paid by the city or was she an employee?

JC: City employee. The city set up these places where people came with their troubles.

BA: Could the kids hang out, and was there one in each neighborhood?

JC: Oh sure. I don't know how many there were but on the East Side on 76th St., one on 68th St. I belonged to both of them.

BA: You mentioned Lenox Hill and that's where you were later on hired to take tickets and there was some kind of a program where they had weekly shows.

JC: That's on 68th St. No, it's a place with the little dances that they used to have.

BA: That's where you tried out your Peabody for the first time. Were there Friday or weekend dances?

JC: Yeah. Sometimes it was that way.

BA: This Miss Trenholm, what do you remember about her?

JC: Cold, capricious, sensible, very sensible, and if we had a big problem we'd go to her.

BA: Do you remember what kind of problems would take you there?

JC: Oh sure. Well, we had a basketball team and I was a Junior and like the spokesman. Actually, I couldn't put two words together. I remember making a plea for the team, or something like that. I asked if there was any possible, I couldn't think of the word 'chance' so I said any possible 'thing'? She didn't respond that I remember.

BA: So there was that fact that as a kid you were out there and people noticed you. You would get shy or tongue tied.

JC: Yeah.

BA: You were pushed up front, you were the one that became the spokesman.

JC: Fine spokesman.

BA: It seems only when attention was placed on what was happening you either got shy or held back. Did you get stage fright when you started acting at the Settlement House?

JC: Yes.

BA: There too! So even from the very beginning.

JC: Harry never had stage fright. I remember we use to do a Chinese pantomime and he was the leading man. He was supposed to be paddling a canoe. He put make-up on one night and got up there and performed. Don't know what the hell I was doing, but I got up there and did it. I was paddling a canoe on a bare stage.

BA: Harry was a good athlete as well.

JC: He was sort of an all-around guy, although not a fighter. He was a good athlete and a good ball player.

BA: He was interested in acting.

JC: My mother was interested in acting. She was the one who put Harry into the acting group.

BA: She had you pegged for an artist and wanted him to be an actor.

JC: It all depends, it was no stunt at all. I just walked into it.

BA: She was less than happy when you started moving toward acting, she preferred you to stay with your art.

JC: Maybe so.

BA: And your brother Ed?

JC: Ed was a study. He did whatever there was to be done.

BA: And Bill?

JC: Bill was six years younger.

BA: Was the Settlement House a place where you went often, where the guys were?

JC: Yeah. We had basketball for an hour in the gym they had indoors. Harry had big muscles and I was his brother. He was good. It wasn't my sport but I played sometimes.

Jim with brother Bill

BA: Whatever the situation that came up even though Harry was involved, the basketball situation, you were the one they put up as the spokesman. There had to be something, some quality that put you in the forefront. They were all older then you, yet you were the one that had to go and be the leader.

JC: This happened early on. We were starting a basketball team with an Irish gang. They had the players and they had a natural thief by the name of Al Saunders. We never questioned him, he was just one of the guys. He would take shoes, anything that was left in the locker room. That was his business. We both worked at the Friars Club and one of the members of the Friars Club bought a pair of shoes and sent the old ones over to the Club. Al looked at these shoes and just put them on, they were his. But he was a very entertaining fellow. Great cocksman, if half the stories he told were true. Typical red-faced Irish with gall written all over him.

BA: How old were you at the time?

JC: Nineteen.

BA: So all the actors and show business people were there at the Friars Club in those days.

JC: They weren't actors. They were just people, different kinds of people.

BA: Our association with the Friars today is show business.

JC: Show business, yeah. George Jessel was a human being apart. Front and center. I met him when he was a member of the Club. I didn't know him at all. I met him later on in Hollywood.

George Jessel

CHAPTER 8

Show Business

BA: With your father passing it's almost as if you were liberated. You were free to move on in your life to something else at that point.

JC: Yeah, I guess moving forward.

BA: Was the term 'show business' used in those days?

JC: Show business.

BA: I was in college at the time. It looked like I was going into show business with my partner Buzz. My mother said, "Your partner Buzz, is he going to go into the show business too?" She said 'the show business.'

JC: Goddamn glad you didn't do it. Everyone that makes it has to be lucky. I don't know if they'd lie to me if I didn't have the stuff.

BA: Well, obviously you did. When I started reading through the books and kept coming across the phrase, 'I was just doing a job, it was just a job' I kept wanting to say, 'It can't be it, it can't be it.' And I realized, in fact, that's what you were doing.

JC: Yes, just a job.

BA: I didn't want to believe it, I wanted to look for something grander, something bigger, more profound.

JC: How little we know.

BA: In those days it was food, clothing, and shelter?

JC: That was the whole story. The whole goddamn story. Just grab it as it comes.

BA: There were no extras?

JC: That's right.

BA: Is your recollection of it an 'up' time or a hard time?

JC: It was nothing, not bad, just work. I started working at fourteen. We lived in a flat on 78th St. The main part was 78th, a kitchen, a living room, a bath and three bedrooms.

BA: You shared a room with your brothers?

JC: Yeah that's right.

BA: Which of the brothers were you closest to?

JC: Eddie. Harry was the eldest, I was second eldest, and along came Ed and Bill was the youngest.

BA: Somebody told you about a role that was available.

JC: There was a boy who was stepping out of an act at the 81st St. Theater and Broadway. He told me about it. They're lookin' for a boy. I said, "Okay." So I went up there and he signed me on right away to *Every Sailor*.

78th St Home

Ed, Bill, Jim & Harry

BA: Did you have to audition for him?

JC: No, I didn't have to do any auditioning. The song was so simple. The dance was so simple. Everything about it was so simple that I just walked into it. It was $35 a week. Hey kid, $35 bucks a week!

BA: Was that the most money you'd made up till then?

JC: I was getting $18 a week at Wanamaker's after school. If there was a buck to be made, you made it. And while that buck was being made you were making another buck with some other thing.

BA: And everyone was working and everyone contributed to the central fund.

JC: Oh sure. The old man was dead. Jesus God Almighty, when you think of it, it was tough on the old gal. We did what we could, the boys did to lighten things up. But it wasn't enough.

BA: What were the distinguishing qualities of the brothers in those days?

Every Sailor, 1919

JC: Harry was a born physician, he became one. When Eddie graduated from college Harry said to him why don't you study medicine, Ed? And that was it. Ed would be anything. They eventually became partners. Ed died in '64, Harry in '66.

A family affair. Ed, Bill, Jim, Carrie, & Jeanne

BA: Were you all close?

JC: Oh yeah. God yes.

BA: So it was essentially, if not an intellectual environment.

JC: They were 'on'. Harry was a good football player, baseball player. He was on the swim team at Columbia.

Harry Cagney, 1897, became an obstetrician and had a practice in Queens with his brother and partner Edward, 1902, who also became a doctor, a general practitioner. Both moved their practice to California to join the rest of the family. William Cagney, 1905, went to CCNY and became business manager and financial advisor throughout his brother Jim's life. Jeanne, 1919, graduated from Hunter College at age 19, cum laude. She held her own as a lovely actress and appeared in four films with her brother Jim. Yankee Doodle Dandy 1942, The Time of Your Life 1948, A Lion Is in the Streets 1953, Man of a Thousand Faces 1957.

BA: So you took this job and put on a wig and female clothing. You went on stage and watched the others and learned from them.

JC: Stole steps constantly.

BA: Were you aware of your presence on a stage in front of an audience? Do you remember that, that feeling?

JC: Oh yeah, sure. It didn't mean a thing.

BA: This was coming off the army days so that female impersonators were fairly common in those days. I guess from army shows.

JC: Oh no. They were not common.

His 'Bill'

BA: Who would come to the shows, regular people?

JC: Anybody. Oh yes, sure.

BA: And the performers were all guys. Was it done in a campy style or done straight out?

JC: Guys. There was no attempt to be girlish. Except there were boys. There was five and five. Five guys and five fags.

BA: Was there a point to the balance?

JC: No. They needed, well, they'd do anybody who'd put on a wig.

BA: How long did that show last?

JC: Two months.

BA: You made a fair amount of money, $35 bucks a week. Brought it home and put it in the kitty.

JC: Oh sure, for the kitty.

BA: When did you actually move out of the house?

JC: About that time. I got a room. There wasn't any great thought given to it, you know.

BA: Well, it's just that you were the first to move out from the family. You were close to your brothers.

JC: Yes, a close-knit family. Harry stayed on and Ed and Bill. They were all in school at the time and Jeannie was there by then.

BA: By then you were going with Nellie.

JC: We were just splitting up.

BA: Did any specific thing cause that?

JC: No, I was in show business.

BA: Was that some sort of a stigma?

JC: I don't know. It was a way of living.

BA: Drifted apart?

JC: Yes.

BA: The next lady of any consequence was Willie then.

JC: Yes, My Bill.

Early Vaudeville

CHAPTER 9

Stage Fright

BA: How about this business of your nervous stomach prior to performances?

JC: That stayed with me always. I opened the act in Kanke, Illinois. We did a dancing act and finally we did a talking act with dancing. (*loudly*) WWWHOOO OWWW. (*laughter*). You would think anybody getting that sick, would get the hell out of the business.

BA: That's what I figured.

JC: No. Never thought of it.

BA: The thought did cross my mind last night.

JC: What would you want with it?

BA: When I was about ten or eleven I was visiting my aunt and uncle in Westhaven, CT where there was an amusement park. I was deathly afraid of the roller coaster and I would get on that ride and say "Here we go again." I'm still afraid of roller coasters.

Working together in a Vaudeville act

Jack & Mary Benny

JC: Amazing, you're right.

BA: Did it ease up a bit when you went to Hollywood?

JC: I didn't have any sickness there at all. I was more composed. It left me. Maybe it was because of the contempt I felt for the people around me.

BA: All you had to do is act.

JC: He can't do anything either. (*both laugh*)

BA: Did it hit you before going on stage or when you were on stage?

JC: Before I went on.

BA: Every night?

JC: Oh sure.

Mrs. Cagney (Willie): We didn't have a dime and we were trying to do an act and we had to keep a bucket in the wings to run off and throw up into and come back and read the line. (*laughter*)

BA: So it was always there?

Mrs. Cagney: Even more so then. But it's a funny thing, that was always stage work, it seems to me. The movies there was none of that. Just shows in the vaudeville days. Movies never bothered him. Isn't that odd? Of course he didn't have an audience, he only had a crew around, electricians and what not. They didn't bother him in the slightest.

JC: We were heading to Waukegan, Illinois, Jack Benny's hometown, and when I went on there, I threw up first, of course, did the act came off and threw up again.

Frank Fay

BA: Did you know Benny in those days? Was he established?

JC: Oh yeah, sure. But he was an imitation of Frank Fay. Mary, his wife, was in the act with him.

JC: See, she never liked to perform, you know. She was nervous. That made two of us throwing up.

BA: You mean you were on the same bill at the same time?

JC: Yeah.

BA: As she had the same infliction.

JC: I don't know. But afterwards she told me she was nervous all the time.

Frank Fay was a vaudeville comedian and film actor. He was the first to start what stand-up comedy is today. He was married to Barbara Stanwyck from 1928-1935.

BA: Were you with Willie at that time. Did you and Jack stay friends through the years.

JC: Oh sure. The day before he died, he came over to the house. He was a nice man. They were giving me, whatever the hell it was, an award. Later, he called up, "I got to see you before I go Jim." I said, "You've got plenty of time." He said, "Oh yeah, like hell." He knew. Can't save him.

CHAPTER 10

Panic Island

BA: I'm trying to think of the name, there was a place you mentioned where actors used to go to when they were out of work. They would gather and stand on the island.

JC: Panic Island.

BA: That's a great name. What do you remember about Panic Island?

JC: Just that I had some friends there.

BA: So all the guys that were not working would go there? Sorta like the Schwab's of the time.

JC: Oh sure. I suppose. I've never been in a Schwab's.

BA: You didn't miss too much. You were working so you wouldn't go to Schwab's. Was it a street?

JC: No, you know the street. You know where Father Duffy's statue is.

BA: Do you know how it got the name?

With Joan Blondell in *Maggie The Magnificent*, 1929

JC: No. I don't know. No great to do about it, just a place to hang out.

BA: In between triumphs, huh?

JC: Always in between triumphs.

BA: Did you have an agent in those days?

JC: Oh sure. William Morris.

Maggie The Magnificent

BA: Did you go find an agent or did they come get you?

JC: No, if I remember rightly he was the one who got the contract with Warner Brothers. I didn't give a shit. Never.

BA: By then you were working with Joan Blondell.

Even in his first role he had 'it' in *Sinner's Holiday*, 1930

JC: Yes, we were in 2 shows: *Maggie The Magnificent* and *Penny Arcade*.

BA: Did Jolson have something to do with it?

JC: Yeah. He saw the show and bought it.

BA: Was he associated with the Morris office? That was the connection. So your first representation then was a result of the contract which Warner Bros. wanted you to sign.

JC: Yeah. *Sinner's Holiday*.

BA: You didn't have an agent when you were on Broadway?

JC: Chamberlain Brown. I was with them the longest, I guess, and when they had to represent me, they didn't.

Jim & Joan in *Penny Arcade*, 1930

BA: Because of the studios?

JC: They had no interest in incurring the wrath of the studio.

BA: That's what I assumed.

JC: Maybe so, I don't know.

Penny Arcade

Maggie The Magnificent - Cort Theater, opened October 21th, 1929 - November 29th 1929. 32 performances. Role - Elwood......James Cagney

Penny Arcade - Fulton Theater, opened March 3rd, 1930 - March 31st, 1930 24 performances Role - Harry Delano......James Cagney

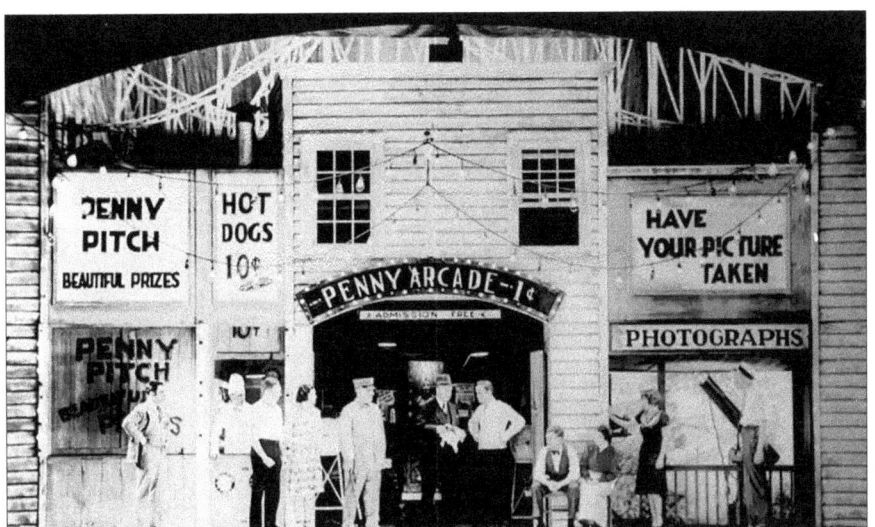

Penny Arcade

Maggie *The Magnificent* Playbill, 1929   *Penny Arcade* Playbill, 1930

George Abbott

CHAPTER 11

Broadway

BA: A FACE APPEARED on the screen the other night at the Tony's. (*the Tony Awards aired on June 3, 1983*) Apparently you did work with George Abbott many years ago.

JC: Oh sure. He staged *Broadway*. I took up the cudgels of understudying the lead and that was when I was fired.

BA: He looked pretty good the other night.

JC: He looked fine, yeah.

BA: Did they do a film of that show, *Broadway*?

JC: Oh yeah.

BA: That had to be a blow. Was it?

JC: No. Willie got mad, not me, so what? She said, "I'd like to burn down your goddamn office". It must have been a severe strain on Jed Harris, but he didn't show any emotion about it at all.

BA: What was he like?

JC: Jed Harris? Oh shit. Prick. He had everybody there too.

BA: So it was a forerunner of things to come, you knew the type.

JC: Oh sure.

JC: I'll bet.

Mrs. C: I was going to England. I got $50 a week you know, just to be along. Understudying one of the gals, a bit part. And just to get the trip and to be with Jim, we had given up the apartment. The trunk was on the ship going over and I couldn't get it out. They gave me 15 cents to go buy another dress, 'cause I didn't have any clothes.

BA: Who delivered the blow, was it George Abbott?

Mrs. C: Oh no. Nothing to do with Abbott. I heard he came on last night at 85-years old.

BA: That's right. He looked wonderful.

Mrs. C: He did.

BA: He looked great. He came running down the aisle.

Mrs. C: Running?

BA: Yeah, He won a Tony Award for *On Your Toes*.

Mrs. C: Oh God. That's wonderful. We visited him up in Westport one time. We were called up to his office at two in the morning and told us that we were out.

BA: What was his attitude?

The Early Years

Jed Harris

Mrs. C: It didn't bother him any.

BA: That's what Mr. C. was saying.

Mrs. C: Just one of those things. Get rid of those actors, you know.

BA: So give me a little on Jed Harris who was a giant in the theater.

JC: He said Jed Harris would never produce a flop, next one flopped (*laughter*).

Passport to England, 1926

BA: Is he the one that told you that you were out?

JC: Oh no. He was out of town. He didn't come around at all.

BA: Who did tell you?

JC: Crosby Gaige. He was partners with Harris.

BA: Did they give you any sort of explanation?

JC: No, I was just a lowly actor. Get rid of the son-of-a-bitch.

BA: Do you have any idea why it did happen, 'cause you were doing well in the part.

JC: Nobody could have made it, you see. I was a hoofer, the guy (Lee Tracy) that was in the part was a hoofer. And I played him like a hoofer. They didn't want that. The Tracy traits he had was so established in their minds, no one could have made it.

P36-*Broadway* Playbill, 1926-27

BA: It had to be like Tracy was playing it.

JC: He did that, actually. But he was surprised.

Mrs. C: We were at a nightclub at two in the morning. We were celebrating our trip, saying goodbye to us which was nice. Oh, I tell you, all the actors were up in arms that time.

BA: There had actually been a performance that night.

Mrs. C: Oh, but not with him. It was with that fellow Lee Tracy.

Broadway was at the Broadhurst Theater and ran from September 16, 1926 thru February 11, 1928. 603 performances. Jim was understudy to the lead.

Mary Law, Mary Boland, Jim in *Women Go On Forever*

Mrs. C: Jim didn't say a word. I was the one to say, "I'd like to burn your goddamn office to the ground."

BA: You told him that?

Mrs. C: Oh yeah, I said it. I think he said, "I don't blame you Mrs. Cagney." We'd given up our apartment, our clothes had gone on the ship, everything, so it was quite a thing. God. It was such a blow and the whole bit was so awful that it was a terrible period. But thank God we were young at the time. Show business.

BA: What year could that have been then?

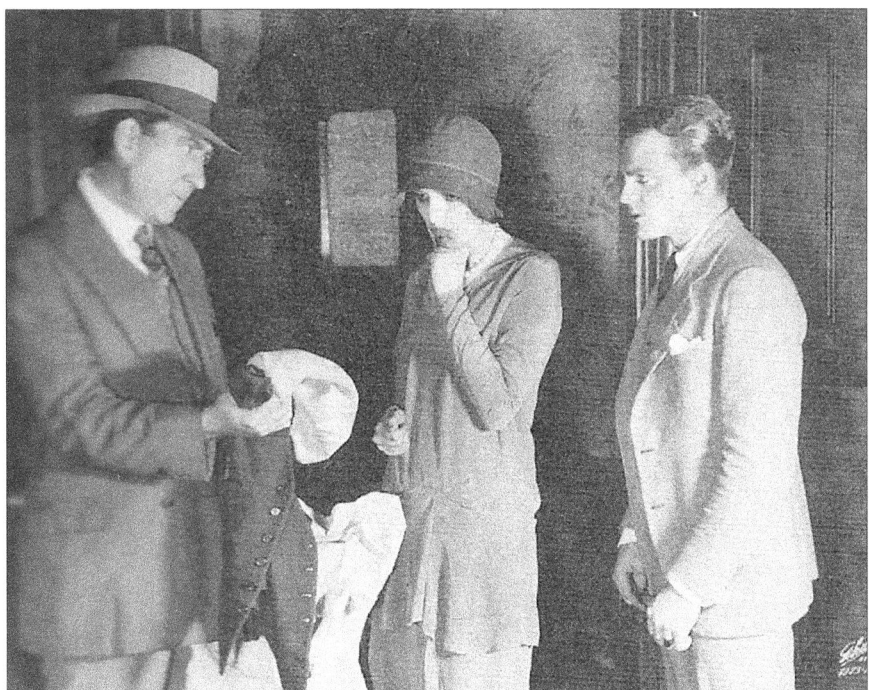

Women Go On Forever

Mrs. C: 1927. And they took Lee Tracy. Anyway, then they were gonna make me go. They thought that would do the trick of getting him, or so that he wouldn't get the run of the play contract. So they put us in understudying *Broadway* that was going at the time. Backstage we had to hang around every day, every night, every matinee. They gave me the part that I was understudying, it was a small bit, but she was about six-feet tall and skinny as a rail and I had to get into those clothes. You should have seen me.

BA: So you did go on for her, then?

Mrs. C: I went on for her one night because she was on the subway and something happened and she couldn't get there and the audience was hooting, applauding and carrying on and I had to go on. I hadn't rehearsed the lines or anything. They just pulled me around the stage, go here, go there, say this. Oh, it was just awful. I look back and laugh but then, it was so awful.

Women Go On Forever Playbill, 1927

BA: I know he told me that Harris was not unlike some of the Hollywood producers.

Mrs. C: He was a horrible man. And then later on, years later, I sat next to him at the Hacketts, friends of ours at the Vineyard. Oh boy, what didn't I say to him (*laughter*).

BA: So essentially then you had to start over here in New York. You had to start from scratch again.

Mrs. C: Scratch. Jim got *Women Go On Forever* right after that.

BA: Which was a very big thing.

Mrs. C: Yeah, in those days. Mary Boland had a big name.

BA: He told me that the first night he handed in his own notice.

Mrs. C: Yes, he did. He said, "I'm no good at this." The thing did something to him and he lost his confidence, you know.

BA: And John Cromwell called him in.

Mrs. C: And said you're doing it exactly as I want you to do it. Exactly. So that helped. He went on and then got easier in it. Guess he was in for the whole play.

BA: It's an interesting title, *Women Go On Forever*. Do you remember what it was about?

Mrs. C: Daniel wrote it.

Women Go On Forever played at the Forrest Theater. September 7, 1927 thru December 1927, 117 performances. Jim's role was Eddie. Playwright Daniel N. Rubin

Mrs. C: It's too bad that I haven't got all those scrapbooks. I kept scrapbooks.

BA: You did?

Mrs. C: I have 'em at home.

BA: I know Marge talked to Bill Greenblatt about the possibility of going over to the house and getting some of them.

Mrs. C: You mean going over to the California house? Without me there, it's kind of tough.

BA: Well, we'll get you there.

At their home on Hillcrest, 1932

Mrs. C: (*laughs*) Oh I love it out there. I love the house. You've never been there?

BA: I was there one night to pick Marge up the night we went to see Liza Minnelli. I was in the house just for a few minutes.

Mrs. C: Oh, so you came up through the court to the door.

BA: I could sense it's a special place.

Mrs. C: It's a lovely, beautiful place.

BA: Did you move into that right after the Hillcrest house?

Mrs. C: Yes, we built that in '39 and then like fools, we went away to New York for some reason or other, and a lot of things were done wrong which we had to change when we got back. Never go away when you're building.

BA: That's true. You built it to your own specs?

Mrs. C: Yeah.

BA: That's why it has that Eastern feel to it, distinctive.

Mrs. C: Irish stone house.

BA: Really lovely. Maybe this afternoon, if you're up to it, maybe the three of us can sit down and chat. It might be interesting. He's feeling good today. We started talking about the actual making of the film and it's beginning to gel now, it's beginning to make sense.

Mrs. C: He must be feeling better.

BA: I accidentally touched his foot, and it didn't hurt this morning.

He had a wonderful idea when I first walked in this morning. What he wants to do, and these are his words. "We'll invade the theaters and we'll do all the old songs." We started talking about the notion of getting something like the Roger Chorale, songs of the century.

Mrs. C: He has good ideas. I didn't know he was thinking of those things.

BA: It rained real hard last night.

Mrs. C: I know it did, thunder and lightning. I was awake last night, because we lost two horses to lightning. They didn't have harnesses or metal on them. Shoes though, they had horseshoes on.

BA: Were they out in the pasture?

Mrs. C: Yeah.

BA: Boy, that came out of nowhere last night. So maybe we can give him a little lunch pretty soon and then around two or three, I'll come back.

Mrs. C: Three.

BA: And we'll do another one.

Mrs. C: Ok.

BA: It might be fun for the three of us to sit in there. You'll spark each other, you'll see.

Mrs. C: It's such a crazy place. Things that have been going on that's made me just dizzy.

BA: (*JC is back*) Mrs. C. has kind of filled me in a little on the Broadway incident with Jed Harris.

Coldwater Canyon Home Beverly Hills

Mrs. C: What was the name of that man?

JC: Crosby Gaige.

Mrs. C: He's the one I said I'd like to burn your goddamn office to. Remember? And you never uttered a word.

BA: Clothing was on board, you'd given up the apartment.

Mrs. C: Our trunks went over. And they gave us a little bit of money to buy me a dress. I had nothing except what I was wearing. And where did we go then?

JC: We took the Shumlin apartment.

BA: Herman Shumlin, in the hotel?

Herman Shumlin was a Broadway Director from 1927-1974.

Mrs. C: We did. I don't remember his apartment.

BA: Were you a quick study of lines?

JC: Yeah.

Jim late 20's

BA: You mentioned a couple of directors that you worked with on the stage. Cromwell was one.

JC: John Cromwell, yeah. Good man. He directed *Women Go on Forever.*

BA: Which essentially happened as a result of losing the *Broadway* part.

JC: I guess so.

BA: With Mary Boland.

JC: I gave my notice the opening night of the show.

BA: Why was that?

JC: I was lousy in my estimation.

BA: You gave your own notice?

JC: Yeah. So George Abbott and Cromwell called me in after the show one night and said, "Can we talk for a few minutes?" I said, "Sure." He said, "I want you to take the notice back." I asked why and he said, "You're exactly what we need." We went from there and I said, "Are you serious?" He said, "Yes." And I said, "I'll go back where I belong." He said, "Where's that?" I said, "Vaudeville." He said, "No, you can play this part better than anyone we can gather." I said, "OK" and he tore up my notice. I got great notices. How little we now ourselves, you know.

The Palace Theatre

CHAPTER 12

The Palace

BA: Playing in the Palace was, to me, it was called, "The Palace," which conjures up an image of a palace. It was like playing before royalty.

JC: That's right.

BA: Did you get there?

JC: Yeah, one Sunday. I was in the *Grand Street Follies*. They invited us to play the Palace on Sunday.

BA: Was that the first year or the second year of the *Grand Street Follies of '29*? 'Cause apparently that was a really good show wasn't it?

JC: Sometimes it was good, sometimes it was bad.

BA: The content was that the show where different performers did take-offs on various performers of the day. Some doing Mae West etc. In a sense some doing ad lib performances or were the acts set.

Mildred Keats

"The A.B.C. of Traffic:"-The Dancing Cop - *Grand Street Follies of '29*

JC: No. All set.

BA: Do you remember what you did?

JC: Danced. They chose the best acts of the *Grand Street Follies* and put them on at the Palace.

BA: What was the feeling playing there, did you get some sort of a charge out of it?

JC: Oh no.

BA: But others did?

JC: Sure.

BA: Was your wife working with you at the time?

JC: No. Just me. I'm trying to think who it was fell on her ass. I think it was Mildred Keats. She was a beautiful girl with hair on her tits (*laughter*).

Grand Street Follies of '29

BA: Was she a singer, dancer?

JC: Beautiful dancer, yeah. Trained.

BA: Did you work with her?

JC: She was in the second edition of *Pitter Patter*.

BA: It might be fun to go back and look for specific reviews of the *Grand Street Follies*.

The Early Years

I'm sure I could find it in *Variety* or something.

JC: That was the goal. If you played The Palace, you played the best of it.

Grand Street Follies Playbill, 1929   *Pitter Patter* Playbill, 1920

BA: And yet when you played it, it was nothing special.

JC: Just another theater.

BA: It's still there isn't it?

JC: Yes, on Broadway.

BA: I was just thinking of combining your idea yesterday of going and invading the theaters and doing the songs of yesterday, maybe that's where it should begin at The Palace.

JC: I

Grand Street Follies of 1929 at The Booth Theater opened May 1st, 1929. It ran for 93 performances and closed on July 13, 1929. The following Acts were performed by James Cagney.

Act 2 - The Siege of Troy - Two Youths.......James Cagney & George Heller

Act 3 - Caesar's Invasion of Britain - Force And Montana, Two Dancing Pixies......Mae Noble & James Cagney

Act 7 - I Need You So - Harlequin......James Cagney

Act 11 - A Victorian Victim - A Dominant Male......Dorothy Sands & James Cagney

Act 14 - The A.B.C. of Traffic - The Dancing Cop.......James Cagney

Pitter Patter opened September 28, 1920 thru January 1, 1921 at the Longacre Theater. It ran for 111 performances. Chorus Boy.......James Cagney Chorus Girl.......Frances Willard Vernon

*Jim and Willie married on September 28, 1922 to celebrate their meeting during the play.

CHAPTER 13

Dance School

BA: Discuss the dancing school that you and Willie had in Jersey. It could become a full out musical number with the children.

JC: I doubt it.

BA: (*laughing*) Why do you doubt it?

JC: They couldn't dance.

BA: They couldn't dance, all the more. It could be a funny scene. Did you have anybody there that was progressing.

JC: (*nodding*) NO.

BA: Nobody at all.

BA: You were on a tight schedule, show at night and running the school in the daytime, and commuting.

JC: That's the way it was.

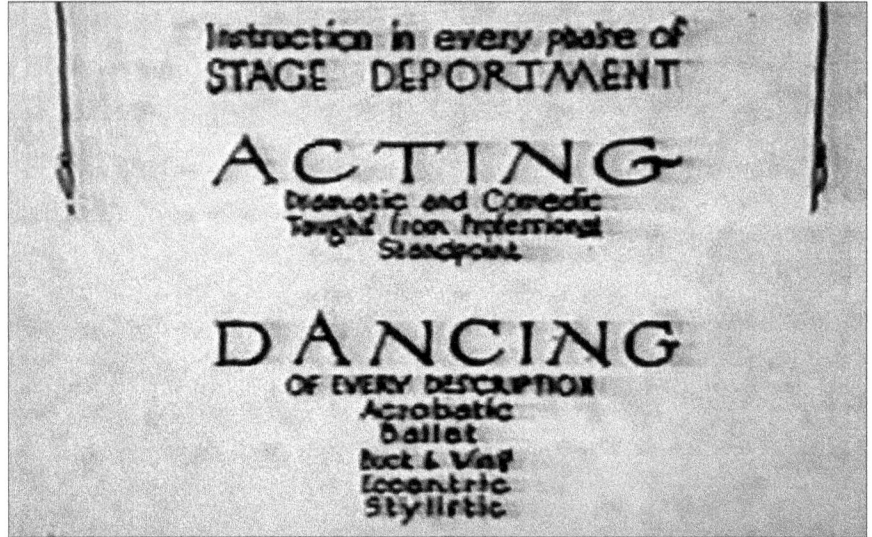

Cagné School of the Dance brochure

BA: Were you teaching?

JC: Oh hell, yes. Taught them stretching of legs. One fellow, a salty Irish kid about 21, he hated everybody. I had a girl, his girl, and I reach out with one hand, so she took the pose. Throwing and catching her and putting her on the ground. I weighed, what around 135 lbs. Why the hell I was doing that, I don't know, showing off.

BA: Was he in the room at the time?

JC: He was there once, yeah. I talked to her about him later. I said, "What's the matter with that guy." She said, "Oh, he's all right. It's just that everybody else is wrong."

BA: It would be nice if you could say, "And that man today is...."

JC: He's nobody. He's still probably going around saying I studied with him.

Jim mid 20's

BA: So you were actually teaching older kids in their teens and twenties?

JC: Oh sure. The youngsters didn't know anything.

BA: They had already done something in the business.

JC: Yeah, they played the benefits. You know, the church benefits.

BA: Did it run the gamut, was it tap?

JC: Oh sure. I taught them everything. Couldn't do anything myself, but I taught them everything.

BA: You must have been able to do something, because you choreographed too. Somebody picked up something that you were doing right.

JC: Well I showed them how to do an eccentric time step.

BA: Country time step?

JC: Eccentric time step. Taking an ordinary time step and doing it with eccentric moves.

BA: Was that your own innovation?

JC: I guess so. I was never happy with what was handed to me. I always did something else with it.

BA: What would you consider an eccentric move?

JC: I'd have to show it to you.

BA: Maybe soon, huh? But it was a contortion of the whole body.

JC: Oh sure.

BA: So you would begin with just the time step and you'd show them that.

JC: We could start off by showing a time step and then evolving into these other various steps.

Mrs. C: Did he tell you that some couple we knew lived in Plainfield, New Jersey. Ed Miller had a little girl and she wanted to learn tap dancing. We had a school in Elizabeth, New Jersey, starved to death, but we had it.

BA: Did you move there?

Mrs. C: Oh no. We lived on 108th Street in the Village.

BA: Then you would travel every day to Elizabeth?

Mrs. C: Every day we would get up and go to the subway and take the ferry over to the school. Every morning and on Saturday's too. Get up at 5:00 a.m. Get over there and teach til noon, get back on the subway and the ferry take the subway up to the Boothe Theater. We didn't have time to change clothes and then go on the stage and to show in the *Grand Street Follies*.

BA: You were teaching kids at the same time? What were you teaching them?

Mrs. C: Oh yes. Tap. Put on a show for the mothers. They would come and fight over their daughter having a solo, or something, who couldn't do a backbend. Oh, we went through all that.

BA: Then you'd take that whole trip back to go to the *Grand Street Follies*.

Hy Rubin sketch of Jim during the *Grand Street Follies*, 1928

Mrs. C: Then we'd do the show, go out to eat, did the matinee on Saturday, then go out and eat, run back and do the night show and then go home and go to bed. But we were young then. (*laughs*) Makes a heck of a difference.

(Just a Little Love Song), With Lily Lubell, *Grand Street Follies of '28*

Hal Le Roy

BA: How long did that routine last?

Mrs. C: It was quite a few weeks, four months.

BA: What were the parts in the *Follies*. Were there speaking parts?

Mrs. C: Not really. Well, Jimmy had a part.

BA: Was it a revue kind of show?

"A Party on the S.S. ILE DE France, In Port" with Jean Crittenden, *Grand Street Follies of '28*

Mrs. C: It was very popular in those days. He danced with a big gal, Lily Lubell. He's got a photo of it.

BA: Do you have memorabilia from that period?

Mrs. C: Not much. You never think of those things.

BA: What does exist is here or back on the Coast?

Mrs. C: Oh, I imagine it must be back at the Coast 'cause we didn't get anything here 'til '55. Jim bought this land in '55, there was no house here and we lived for a few weeks where the horseman is. In that little white house over there. But we never thought of living up here.

BA: You didn't?

Mrs. C: No, it was just a stop gap, you know, one of those things. I was furious when he said he was going to build here. And this place grew. We had no mud room, a kitchen and that was a studio, we painted in there. The dining room, and bedroom he's in now. Just those three rooms.

BA: Really?

Mrs. C: That's all.

BA: It is pretty here.

Mrs. C: It is beautiful. He always was looked at as a NY boy at Warner Bros that we didn't like California, we had you know. He had that court case against Warner Bros and during that time I lost 7 lbs. He couldn't get a job and those things I think turned him against California. He loves the house there, it is a beautiful house. But he liked the East of course, he's from here so maybe that's it.

"From Tango to Taps" with Sophia Delza, *Grand Street Follies '28*

BA: Well, for all of that anguish that he went through, what he did do, he now represents a perception amongst other actors as somebody who was willing to stand up against the big boys.

Mrs. C: Yeah, he did. Oh yeah. He was a fighter. That's why now, because he was such a strong person, definite about everything.

BA: And yet, there was always that, that gentle side of him.

Mrs. C: Kindness.

BA: Great kindness and compassion.

Mrs. C: Oh yes. Absolutely. One of the kindest people you'll ever know.

BA: And it was there even when you first met him.

Mrs. C: Oh yeah.

BA: Which reminds me now, you being a student of the dance, who comes to mind to you today?

JC: Hal LeRoy. He's a great dancer.

BA: You mentioned that you had actually were on Broadway the same time as Bill Robinson?

JC: Oh sure. I worked on a bill with him for two weeks. That's when I stole his time step (*laughter*).

BA: You didn't use it on the same bill?

JC: I guess not. Wouldn't stop me (*laughter*).

BA: Did you have a pretty good relationship with him?

JC: Very few people who could touch him. Very few. Couldn't get to him.

BA: Was he a star by then?

JC: Oh well, yes.

BA: Do you remember what show you were in with him?

JC: No, regular vaudeville show.

BA: Now vaudeville is something that we don't see today. The closest thing probably to it was the early '50's that we would call the television variety show. Sullivan was that essentially vaudeville. There was nothing connecting the acts.

JC: Except that fuckin' dunderhead Sullivan.

BA: (*laughs*) There's a hidden talent here, I see, you just did him. So we can do something with you and Willie. You would think of an act, a turn and work on and then present it as such.

JC: What we can do is Willie and I can do a double and what you can do is cut right in the middle with the other girl. You'll see she's a good dancer. Like a Palace bill and she shows some dances and we stole those steps.

BA: Any particular one of those stolen dances that you remember?

JC: Everyone that I did that I stole, I varied.

Hal Le Roy (December 10, 1913 – May 2, 1985) was an American dancer, actor, and singer appearing on stage, in film, and on television.

Grand Street Follies of 1928 at The Booth Theater opened May 28th, 1928. It ran for 144 performers and closed on October 1st, 1928. The following Acts were performed by James Cagney:

Act 2 - 1928 - Jimmie......James Cagney

Grand Street Follies Playbill, 1928

Act 5 - From Tango to Taps - The Tap Dancers......James Cagney & Sophia Delza

Act 7 - Just a Little Love Song - 1928 Couple.......James Cagney & Lily Lubell

Act 18 - On The Honeymoon Deck, Bound For Africa - The Blues Singers......James Cagney & Jean Crittenden

Act 19 - Romeo & Juliet - James Cagney

Dances by James Cagney

CHAPTER 14

Invade the Theater

BA: When you said invade the theater's what does that mean invade? Just go from theater to theater?

JC: Yeah. We'd invade the theaters and sing all the old songs. The favorites two years ago. (*Laughs*)

BA: Put a singing group together.

JC: Yeah, I'll find them.

BA: I'm sure you will. Now when you say the songs of long ago, it's going to be 50 and 75 years ago.

JC: Right.

BA: The songs of the century, how about that?

JC: You don't know what the hell they're gonna think. Certainly, they thought the same. Wait a minute, here's a company with songs from the same period. I think it's better. Sing the good songs. The theater is unlighted, no, it's lighted. Curtain goes up and in come a troupe of eight guys who sing. And they sing all the old songs a hundred years old or more.

At the piano

With Bill playing the old songs

BA: To invade the theaters and do the songs of the century.

Marge Zimmerman: Isn't that wonderful? You gonna cry about it?

JC: Sure.

MZ: You're such a sweetheart, Jim. You're willing to narrate part of this, Jim?

Allie Wrubel

BA: Sure, that would be wonderful to actually involve yourself in front of the camera as well as behind.

JC: I'll try to.

MZ: You can do it kid.

BA: Do you know who the Roger Wagner Chorale is?

JC: Oh yeah, I know them. I worked with them years ago.

BA: Did you really? In what capacity?

JC: Some picture that we had to have a big chorus.

BA: Maybe that would be a group that we could develop this thing with Roger.

JC: Yeah, sure.

BA: It happens that I'm going to be associated with them on another project in the coming months. That's why his name was in my mind.

JC: In vaudeville they say, "Show 'em where the hell they stand."

BA: Exactly. And we take our lead from Mr. Shakespeare who did it rather well. You know the play within the play notion?

JC: Yeah sure.

BA: So that would be the basic structure.

Roger Wagner Chorale did the score's song in The Gallant Hours, 1960. Roger also composed and conducted the score.

BA: Do you play the piano?

JC: A little bit.

BA: Have you been there recently? To a piano?

JC: No. Not in a couple of years.

BA: Do you pick it up by ear?

JC: Yeah, guitar too.

BA: If we do this other thing, and we will do it, going out on stage with a group and singing songs. At some point it would be wonderful if you would actually go to the piano and pound one out yourself. We're going to do this. This is no pie in the sky stuff.

BA: (*Mrs. C. walks in*) I asked him if he plays, and he said he hadn't played in a while, but I can just see at one point during the stage presentation, him actually going to the piano and singing. It'd be wonderful.

Mrs. C: What's that tune he used to sing?

BA: Which one?

Mrs. C: Oh, it's a dirty song. (*Bill laughs*) Oh, I've got to ask him. Maybe it will come to me.

BA: We'll do a triple this afternoon. Maybe the three of us will just sit here. You two can bounce off of each other.

Mrs. C: Allie Wrubel taught him the song. Oh, he wrote a lot. In fact, he got the Oscar for Disney's *Zip-A-Dee-Doo-Dah* in 1946.

Elias Paul 'Allie' Wrubel was a friend and roommate at Columbia University in 1918.

CHAPTER 15

Presence

DO YOU KNOW THE contemporary performer named Michael Jackson? He asked me what I was doing now and I told him I was working with Martin Sheen. And that I just returned from spending six weeks with Cagney. He seemed interested, but it was the manner in which he responded to Cagney's name when I mentioned it, that would reveal volumes about his inner self. He paused for a beat, before saying, "Cagney!" He good." As a performer himself, he was ranking another.

BA: Yesterday, I had occasion to call a business associate of mine who had come to me with an idea which I've since developed for public broadcasting. It's a pretty interesting idea but has nothing to do with any of this. The guy is in his mid-thirties. He's a public relations man for Rock n' Roll bands and he's quite removed from all of this. I told him I was here and that I was working with you. There was this long silence and he said, "Would you tell Mr. Cagney that he gave me hours and hours of real enjoyment over the years,". This is an extension of what you were saying. Not only how little we know of ourselves, but how little we know of how we touch so many other people in life.

JC: Probably one of those who remember the old days of gangsterism. There aren't very many of them.

BA: Well his favorite was *Yankee Doodle Dandy*. He says he's watched it 30 times on television.

JC: Yeah?

BA: There's just no way for us to know how or what we're doing that touches others.

JC: True. Hard to know.

BA: So it's our responsibility to do it as best we can.

JC: Yes. Always the best.

BA: Did that type of thing happen in those days?

JC: Sure. It was happening right from the very start. We knew what we thought when they performed in front of a microphone. They had all the presence.

BA: Would George Jessel be one of those, he had it?

JC: Oh yeah, sure. I couldn't understand this. Where do they have this kind of presence? When they'd never done anything.

BA: And yet, when you got on the stage, you had it too.

JC: No.

BA: Ah hah! I see what you're saying now. So yours came from another place? So there's different kinds of ways of connecting with an audience.

JC: It's always something different in their performance. Their jumping into this act tomorrow morning. So I would step in and shit in my pants, of course (*laughter*). Struck me then, it's a hell of a way to make a living.

BA: But you did it.

JC: Oh sure.

BA: So when you say 'step into this act,' can you give me an example of a kind of act? The different things that spark performers on the stage that allow them to connect with an audience.

JC: Difference was that the guys who knew how to do it, you walk on and in, no fear.

BA: But the fear came from thinking that you couldn't do it. Once you were out there doing it, there was no fear.

JC: No. You had the part set in mind. Do what's required in a sketch. What have you got to lose? You get up there spouting, let it happen.

BA: I was talking to Mrs. Cagney this afternoon about the fact that, if you were on the stage and you became successful, people respond to you. The response is immediate.

Toto the Clown

CHAPTER 16

Flash Acts

BA: WATCHING THE TONY Awards the other night they would have these ensemble numbers where there are 10-15 dancers on stage. There was always one or two with their energy level was so great that they would just kind of stand out. It would be marvelous to find young people to recreate, as you say, those old acts, those old bills.

JC: That's right.

BA: Suppose I were to say make me up an ideal bill from top to bottom?

JC: I wouldn't know where to begin.

BA: Who would you open with? You have your choice, anybody.

JC: No, you haven't got your choice.

BA: You don't. Why?

JC: There's a #1 Act, #2 Act, #3 Act.

BA: Ok, who's your choice to start with #1 Act.

Chappelle & Stinnette

JC: There would be an opening number, then the comedian of the first act would start something, like have a blind horse or something.

BA: So the first was generally a comic?

JC: He was a physical act.

BA: Who would you get to be the opening physical act?

JC: They're all dead.

BA: We know that, but if we gave them a call, sort of a command performance. I would like to put together the all-time vaudeville bill.

JC: Toto the Clown.

BA: We can get into *Variety* and look up his reviews and we'd find out what he did and could recreate it as best we could. Who's next?

JC: A piano act. Chappelle & Stinnette. They were colored people.

BA: What kind of music did they play?

JC: Modern music. He'd do this, she'd do this, and she said, "I wish you would, I wish you would."

BA: So they did a little bit too, not just playing piano.

JC: Yeah. There are people around who are worth laughing at.

BA: The comics, the great comics.

JC: Oh sure. Jack Pearl. Cooled.

BA: Cooled?

JC: He died.

BA: (*laughing*) I wasn't ready for that phrase (*laughter*). Who else in vaudeville comes to mind?

Jack Pearl

JC: Going back 50 years ago, Burns & Frabito.

BA: Not George Burns.

JC: Oh no. This is an Italian, Frabito, he had syphilis and he sang. The Italian and George Burns played the Palace. I don't know where the hell I was, doing something in the area and saw the show. I jumped and the balloons exploded. He was selling balloons and he did that (*showing how they exploded*) and George would say to the other guy, "Vito, I think he was Dutch. Me no touch. You touch. Me no touch."

BA: That was the act.

JC: Yeah. And the balloons would go off and 'I thinkayou touch."
(*laughter*)

Toto the Clown was played by Armando Rovello. Actor/vaudevillan known for The Vaud-O-Mat 1936. He died in 1938 at age of 49.

Chappelle & Stinnette Revue, Vaudeville and Musical Comedy from 1912-1932.

Jack Pearl a Vaudeville performer turned Broadcaster introduced the character Baron Munchauser. Famously saying, "Vass you dere, Sharlie?"

BA: So we have Toto, Chappelle & Stinnette.

JC: Followed by a sketch.

BA: The classic all-time sketch would be?

JC: Burns & Frabito. I played on a bill with them and the second time we started to dance, the two of us, Burns and I, he propositioned me (*laughter*).

BA: I think you better explain yourself. You mean to join the act?

JC: Oh no. He wanted to take me out and have me do him.

MZ: Oh, so he was a fag?

JC: Oh no.

MZ: Well, what the hell are you talking about? Somebody propositioned you. What did he proposition you for? Jamsie tell me what he wanted you to do. To polish your shoes?

JC: No. Well, he was to be the chicken.

Donald Kerr

MZ: The chicken?

JC: Yeah. You don't understand that?

MZ: No, I sure as hell don't. What was he a farmer?

JC: No. No. He would permit me to do things that normal people don't do.

JC: We're just putting the act together. A physical act, a piano act, we've got a sketch and a comedy act.

BA: Comedy act follows the sketch?

JC: Yeah. Burns & Frabito.

BA: Followed by?

JC: A flash act.

BA: How would you define a flash act?

JC: I won't tell you (*laughter*).

MZ: What the hell's a flash act.

JC: More than two people. Donald Kerr & Co.

BA: Which consisted of?

JC: Half a dozen people, singers and dancers.

BA: And they'd really come out and cut it up.

JC: Some were soul singers.

BA: Was there a specific kind of song?

JC: Any popular song.

BA: Sing and dance and acrobatics.

JC: They both came on and they brought Donald Kerr on to be a specialty dancer in *Pitter Patter*. After one performance they fired him and gave me the job.

BA: So you replaced him?

JC: And I went on and did a dance.

BA: So could we put Jimmy Cagney & Co. as the flash act, or would you want to come on alone later on?

JC: I don't want to appear in this.

> The first entry in the abbreviated scrap book is a yellowed newspaper clipping that is not quite two inches square. It reads:
> "James Cagney has replaced Donald Kerr as a dancing feature with the 'Pitter Patter' company, which opened for a week's run at the Shubert-Riviera Theatre last night. Some time ago it was predicted that this young man's cleverness would result in the recognition of his talent and that more of his work would be brought into the limelight. Now he is rapidly coming to the fore at a pace that eclipses all predictions."
> That is the only scrap book entry of the early years of struggle for recognition on the stage. The next entry, on the same

Review from Jim's personal scrapbook

BA: OK, so we'll put Donald Kerr in just to make up for what we did to him back then. That was really your *matte*.

JC: My what?

BA: Your *matte*. Your environment to do a flash act where you can dance or sing. You were an athlete, you could move, you could jump. Would you put some of the eccentric movement in as well?

JC: Oh sure. Mostly that.

BA: So that was the flash act. It's a lot of socko stuff, one after the other.

JC: That's right. Fearless.

BA: Follow a flash act with what?

JC: Balancing Acrobats: the Japs.

BA: Following the flash act, Wow! You don't give the audience any kind of break.

JC: Fuck the audience. They didn't care. Nobody cared about the audience.

BA: And yet it was their response that made you realize whether you were good or not. Your measure was the audience.

JC: Yeah.

BA: But today we're just picking acts for the ideal bill. A balancing act is that what they were called?

JC: I wish there was a way of describing the Dare Brothers.

BA: Would they come under the heading of a flash act?

JC: No. Two handsome young men. They worked as one.

BA: So you'd follow the flash act with the Dare's.

JC: No. We'd want to get something stronger than them after the flash act. They're not really stronger. They would work in one. Which would give us a chance to change the scenery back behind the curtain, for something with a little production value.

BA: What kind of a setting would a flash act have?

JC: A Palace setting.

BA: A stairway, when you say a Palace setting what do you mean?

JC: Anything granted in the #2 act.

BA: We started talking about the Palace Theater in New York, where everyone aspired to. So that's where we will begin.

CHAPTER 17

The Tonys

BA: THE TONY AWARDS are on tonight, for what it's worth. They're going to have some of the excerpts of some of the plays that are on Broadway. (*laughs*) You're not interested.

It just occurred to me that I was going to ask you about the theater and your feelings about it. Did you ever go back to Broadway after you did movies?

JC: No. Never.

BA: No. You just did movies.

JC: (*Jim looks at the antiques on the mantle*) Isn't this a nice room? Everything in it is second hand or third hand. Antique. That's the oldest piece there. (*points to a sink*) That was the sink in the farmhouse at the Vineyard. A couple a hundred years old. The house was built in 1728.

Jim and Willie loved and collected antiques and had them throughout their homes.

BA: They renamed The Uris Theater on Broadway yesterday to the Gershwin Theater, after George and brother Ira Gershwin. On the Tonys they did a two-hour tribute to George Gershwin and his music. It still stands up today.

JC: That's wonderful. And those two pianists can play the stuff.

BA: So you saw that part? It was Marvin Hamlisch and Peter Nero.

JC: Is he Italian?

BA: Peter Nero, I don't know if he's Italian. I used to work with him, as a matter of fact. He's a New York piano player, wonderful piano player. He plays a lot of the hotels and the clubs around New York. And Hamlisch, of course, is a composer too.

JC: I know him, yeah.

BA: Did you meet Gershwin?

JC: Many, many years ago in the Dark Ages when he was nobody. He had just written *Rhapsody in Blue*.

BA: Really?

JC: Awhile back.

BA: Were you in New York at the time or out on the Coast?

JC: Oh no. Here.

BA: That little sequence where Hamlisch played and it was New York speaking. Ginger Rogers looked pretty good. Did you see her up there singing away? Did you ever work with her?

JC: No, she worked at a different studio.

BA: Lemmon looked pretty good too.

JC: Yeah. A funny fella.

BA: Did you see him the last time you were out on the Coast?

JC: Yeah, I did.

With Edward G. Robinson

CHAPTER 18

Fresh Mutt

BA: IT HAPPENS THAT night you read the reviews the next day, you know that you're a hit or not. This was not necessarily the case in the movies, was it? There was a lag, or could you tell in the rushes or in those first previews?

JC: The thing that in the movie business you see the rushes and you can tell from the rushes if so-so is a hit. Word would come back from the rushes.

BA: Did the attitude change toward you on the lot?

JC: You could tell when the 'smaller people', as Jack put it, had seen the rushes and could be a big man.

BA: Which is where you developed your perception about you can tell how good you are by the other guy.

JC: It's absolutely so.

Bogart in *Angels with Dirty Faces*, 1938

Jean Harlow in *The Public Enemy*, 1930

BA: So it would be from the projectionist, the secretary, people working in the labs that would begin to filter back.

JC: We never saw the people in the labs.

BA: Oh, you never saw them. So, you get the word now that something is obviously happening.

JC: They don't tell you.

BA: They don't tell you that, how you feel about being catapulted into, you know, all of that stuff. And there were other guys and ladies there who had achieved some degree of notoriety. Edward G. Robinson was at the same studio. Had he established himself when you got there.

JC: Oh shit, yes. The first week I was there, he let me know how big he was.

BA: Is that right?

JC: (*imitating Robinson*): Oh yes. (*laughter*)

BA: Who else do you remember letting you know that.

JC: Funny thing, Harry, Harry Seymour, the piano player. He would seem to swell up when you were with him. When you said hello to him (*laughter*). He was too much.

BA: How about Bogart, had he established himself yet?

JC: No. The first 2 or 3 years he was playing two or three parts at the same time. In and out, in and out. He didn't know what the hell he was doing.

BA: Did he get caught up in the ego thing too?

Bette Davis in *Jimmy the Gent*, 1934

JC: Oh yeah. He was a very jealous man. He was up one night at my brother Bill's house. Bill had a living room bar and Bogart use to love to stop by and juice, you know. And it seemed that he told my brother that I was through. My brother slapped him and knocked him down and said, "Now get out of here you son of a bitch, before I take you apart." Bill was a tough guy. Then they got back on good footing again. Everything was all right. But they understood each other where I didn't understand Bogart at all.

BA: Was it insecurity?

JC: I suppose it had something to do with it.

The Irish in Us with Olivia DeHavilland, 1935

BA: There was Robinson, Bogart, yourself. Harlow, was she one of those?

JC: No. She was just a flash in the pan.

BA: Really? How about Robinson, did that relationship change through the years?

JC: Oh yeah. He was married to a very pretty woman, Gladys Robinson. And, she liked to fuck, I guess. And she said, "Did I ever tell you about the time the only time I ever cheated on Eddie? The only time." (*laughter*)

The Strawberry Blonde, 1941

BA: Did you guys get to be close later on in years?

JC: Very flattering. Went on for quite a while. Very flattering to me. He said to me, "Did I tell you that I voted for you for the Academy Award? I'd like you to have a chance of getting it." He didn't have to say that to me, but he did.

BA: Bette Davis?

JC: She didn't like me

BA: No? Why do you think?

JC: I don't know.

BA: Martin said the last time we were driving back down from the farm he was chatting with her about you and she said really good things about you.

JC: She did?

BA: Yeah, that you were one of the few that were sticking your neck out early on. Olivia de Havilland?

JC: Beautiful girl. Frail beauty.

BA: She was living in New Zealand or Australia.

JC: Paris. She was a strange one. You never knew where you stood with her. My grandfather had an expression: "That's the kind of hairpin I am." And I wrote it into the script. It got to be in the final showing, in the rushes. She decided to take that line over and I said, "You can hardly get it." (*laughter*) She said this line might not be right for me. And I said, "Yeah, not in this picture."

BA: At the AFI awards show I remember a little clip of the two of you, and you're sitting on a bench and you're just looking at each other. There's not much talk going on and it was such a marvelous moment, just the two of you together.

JC: *The Strawberry Blonde.*

BA: Have you seen her in recent years?

JC: Just in pictures.

BA: You know she came back a few years ago. She had written a book or something and she appeared occasionally on television. She's still a lovely looking woman.

With friend and co-star Joan Blondell, *Blonde Crazy*, 1931

JC: Beautiful. She was so beautiful I use to laugh right out loud when I saw her on the screen.

BA: Really?

Michael Curtiz directing *Angels with Dirty Faces*

JC: "What are you laughing at?" "I'm laughing at you." "Why?" "You're so beautiful. Nobody has any right to be that beautiful."

Jim had a supporting role in Smart Money 1931, with EGR, who died in 1973.

Jean Harlow: The Public Enemy 1931. She died in 1937.

Bette Davis was with Jim in two movies: Jimmy the Gent 1934 and The Bride Came COD 1941. She died in 1989.

Olivia de Havilland was in three movies with Jim: The Irish in Us 1935; A Midsummer's Night Dream 1935; The Strawberry Blonde 1941.

Humphrey Bogart was in three movies and in each met his demise: Angels with Dirty Faces 1938; The Oklahoma Kid 1939; The Roaring Twenties 1939. He died in 1957.

BA: I know who we haven't talked about. The lady you came to Hollywood with, Joan Blondell.

JC: Nice gal. We had a mutual friend, a fag, who wrapped himself around us, and as time wore on, I use to lift things from him and put them in the pictures.

BA: Do you remember any of them?

JC: A way of saying things.

BA: You have a section in your book about directors where you bring that point up again about all the different kinds of people who. Let's call them directors for now, the ones who have it, the ones who don't. The ones who think that they do and the ones who know that they don't.

JC: You know there was no such person as (Michael) Curtiz, just a director.

BA: I knew a guy like that, Sammy Davis. There was no Sammy Davis, there was just what was up there.

JC: He's a great performer, that kid.

BA: Two years ago he came to Washington D.C. with Martin Sheen and did this show for the Indians for me. He found himself. The person he could never be through all those years, now he is that person. Now there is a Sammy Davis. In addition to being a great performer, there's a person there. You worked *with* your directors, didn't you?

Jack Warner

JC: Yes I did. If they were nice guys. If they were shits I let 'em know it right off the bat.

BA: It's so odd that the studio that you are most associated with was the one that was always at odds with you or you were at odds with them all those years.

JC: Well there was a reason for that, of course. I had something to say and they didn't want to pay for it.

BA: Was Harry Warner any different than his brother Jack?

JC: The same. Different styles. Harry was a tyrant. Jack feared him.

BA: No kidding. Was he older?

JC: Yeah. Jack had an inevitable answer that any kind of company do, "I'm gonna ask my brother."

BA: I don't' recall ever seeing a picture of Harry. I had no idea what he looked like. Did he pass on before Jack?

JC: Yeah.

BA: Where did they come from?

JC: Akron, Ohio. Butchers.

BA: Is that right? They took it and came out to Hollywood.

JC: Yes. Detachment of actors were sent to call on Harry to talk to him about the Guild and when they walked in he said, "Who are you people, I don't know you. You're just little actors." He found out who they were. When I first met Harry, he said, "Hello Mamzer."

Mamzer is a Yiddish word for Bastard.

Joan Blondell was in seven movies with Jim: Sinner's Holiday 1930; Other Men's Women 1930; The Public Enemy 1931; Blonde Crazy 1931; The Crowd Roars 1932; Footlight Parade 1933; He Was Her Man 1934. She died in 1979.

CHAPTER 19

Zanuck

BA: May I mention a name to you and see what it conjures up? Darryl Zanuck.

JC: You haven't got the time. (*laughs*) Ego, Jesus Christ what an ego. He sent me out on a personal appearance tour. And it was interesting because he forgot to tell me how to play. I was no good at the time. I was still a kid, you know. Brand new to the whole thing. And he said, "Take the thing and make it big." And I said, "I'll try to do it." I went out on the road and I found my own way. And it was reported on how he had coached me.

BA: When you say a personal appearance tour, what would you do on those tours, do scenes from the film?

JC: A song and dance routine.

BA: Really? And would they be in association with a film that was going at the same time?

JC: Could have been, yes. Try to get laughs.

BA: Was this a way of building you up?

JC: That's right.

BA: So the studio would actually promote it and send you out. And did they own theaters at the time?

JC: They had their own theaters, yeah.

BA: Did they have people write routines for you?

JC: Yeah. Some of them. Joel Sayre, he was one of the guys. And funnier than I ever was. He was in the 'shovey' stage when he got drunk.

BA: He would shove you? Was he a performer too or writer?

JC: Writer. But he did everything.

BA: Zanuck then would come down and talk to the actors at times.

JC: No. He was afraid of the girls. He had a meeting that we had every day at noon. Same every day.

BA: So it really was across the board, there was them and the actors?

JC: It covered everything. There was nothing they didn't know about acting.

BA: Where did he come from?

JC: Nebraska.

BA: Then what was his relationship to the Warners?

JC: I don't know.

Frank Capra, Jim, Darryl Zanuck, Jack Warner

BA: But they worked together. Did he work for Warner Bros.?

JC: Yeah, he was under contract to Warners.

BA: Then he eventually took over 20th Century Fox. After Skouras passed on.

JC: No, Skouras was still around.

BA: How did he manage that?

JC: Disgusting people.

BA: So were the producers an extension of the studio?

JC: Oh sure. There was Warner and then there were the producers.

BA: They were a part of the 'Executive Branch' as it were. They had a cut on what was coming in. So there was this block and there was 'us lowly actors'?

JC: We were nothing.

BA: Did you have contact with Zanuck on a regular basis?

JC: I was Zanuck's boy, you see.

BA: Was he looking out for you? Was he looking for the right role?

JC: He had discovered me, you see.

BA: That was his perception that he had discovered you. What makes him say that he discovered you?

JC: Because he said so (*laughter*).

BA: That's reason enough.

JC: To him, sure. Well he owned all of us.

BA: He owned you?

JC: I can't believe now how miserable it was. Looking back. Trying to meet the demands of all those people. Young Dick Zanuck knocked on his father's door and said, "You're all washed up."

BA: I wonder what circumstances were there when you say that.

JC: The old man was finished.

BA: Zanuck told him that? Young Zanuck went and told him that?

JC: (*nodding*) Just cut off his father.

BA: To do this film we should do it as it was, as it happened.

JC: Oh sure.

BA: There can be no equivocation about it because you lived it, you saw it, you experienced it.

JC: It didn't seem strange to me at all.

BA: I'm sure it didn't.

JC: He came to me one day and put his arm around my shoulder. I shoved him off.

BA: This is Poppa, not young Dick?

JC: Yeah.

BA: You guys about the same age.

JC: About the same age, maybe a little bit younger.

BA: He was there when you first got there in Hollywood.

JC: He was set.

BA: They must have looked for a certain quality to warrant somebody being a producer.

JC: Ruthless. Do this. There were no redeeming graces. They were mean, arrogant, ruthless.

BA: People like yourself were being thrust out there and that was more the reason why they wanted to feel as if they owned you.

JC: Anything that they had to do, they had to be boss. Strange name (Zanuck) for a guy who would get to be the head of a studio. All Jews and he was the only Gentile.

BA: He was Gentile. I didn't know that.

JC: Oh yes.

BA: So he had to prove himself with his own meddle.

JC: Oh sure.

BA: I'm trying to put myself into that period, in that era in Hollywood. I know what it's like now. A couple of them are heavyweight business men who sort of move into a studio. There wasn't that much of a history.

JC: No, it was too late. Fear of the other guy was coming on up.

BA: You mean within the industry itself?

JC: Yeah sure. There were enormous amounts of money being made.

BA: Just phenomenal.

SAG Portrait of Jim

CHAPTER 20

SAG

BA: You were never a member of the Academy, were you?

JC: No.

BA: Was there a reason for that?

JC: No. Just recently they were going to make me a member of the Academy, a special member.

BA: I just thought that was automatic. The Academy Awards are in fact an extension of the organization.

JC: It's been around longer than the Screen Actors Guild. Shit, yes.

BA: You know who was there the other day when we were at the Waldorf? Gene Autry was there.

Mrs. C: Yeah. I don't think Jim ever worked with him. He made sure he didn't mention Jim too.

BA: He was a little insecure, wouldn't you say?

Mrs. C: They gave Jim such a nice tribute but as a fellow actor, I think he should have just mentioned it. Some didn't come over and go crazy over Jim. I didn't see them going out of their way. And everybody, and all the fans went crazy. Struck me strange. Actors are actors. Jimmy isn't like that.

BA: Now we have to talk about this. The thing is that yesterday when you went to that affair, Sports Luncheon at the Waldorf Grand Ballroom, Sales Executive Club. Present were the New York Yankees, the Los Angeles Angels, numerous sports super luminaries including George Steinbrenner, Gene Autry, Howard Cosell and a few thousand sports fans of all ages. It became apparent again that what I had written early on is very much true. That there is a quality that is obviously inherent in you that makes people respond in a very, a very deep way. It's there. And apparently it was there when you were a kid too. Because those guys up at Sing Sing knew you.

JC: I couldn't have avoided any part of it.

BA: It was destiny. It was inevitable.

JC: Like I say about Ronnie Reagan. He was born to be President. He followed me in as the President of the Screen Actors Guild. I could never make a speech. No good at all, and he was. He could go on for three quarters of an hour without referring to a note. He'd make the speeches and I'd just applaud.

BA: We'd like to move in that direction, when we get to those years. It's a story well worth telling. The story of the formation of the Guild and your participation in it. Yesterday there was a young man there whom you asked me about. His name is John McGuire. He's with the SAG in New York. He's going to dig up some old stuff about the Guild. It could be very important.

SAG Portrait of Ronald Reagan

John McGuire started with the Union in 1969. He held the position of Associate National Executive Director for SAG from 1983 to 2001.

JC: We didn't make much of that at all. But I was very deeply involved.

BA: You say you didn't make much of it?

JC: On no. I knew I was no good at speaking, but when he came along (Reagan) he fell into it. And rightly so. I knew right then and there he was going to be President.

Reagan, Nancy, Jim & Marge at West Point Graduation

BA: You sensed something then?

JC: Yes. Couldn't act worth a goddamn.

BA: You talk to him lately?

JC: About two months ago. I thought he's handled it awfully well so far. It's a fuck of a job.

BA: There's just so much, all those pressures coming in on you from all sides.

JC: Sure.

JC: Lena Horne came to the house one night. The only black in the house. She smiled and took over, she was fabulous.

JC: It was all relaxed after a couple of years.

Discussing SAG

BA: Why do you think that is?

JC: It's just the way people are. Our group against yours. We're gonna get ours, never mind you.

BA: 'Us against them.' When the Guild actually did become a reality, was everyone aware of what had been accomplished?

JC: I don't think anybody realized. They never do.

BA: Bob Montgomery?

JC: Strong man.

BA: Did you ever work with him or did you know him socially?

SAG Ball, 1938

JC: We did *The Gallant Hours*. Bob was director and producer with my Company. And I did a TV show for him in the '50's. (Robert Montgomery Presents: *Soldier from The Wars Returning, 1956*). We were very close. Louie Mayer called him a Communist (laughter). There was a bright man.

BA: He seemed to know where he was at all times. There was a presence about him, wasn't there?

JC: I agree. I remember I'd call him on the phone and we'd talk it all over. 'Communist'. He was not going to be swayed by anything but radical Rightists. He was going to be really Rightist.

BA: You mean in the latter years?

Jim, Bob and brother Bill

JC: Oh no. Even then.

BA: Even *then*!

JC: Oh sure. There was a contradiction of it. Him being so close to me and I'm supposed to be a Leftist.

SAG Portrait Robert Montgomery

BA: Which is what we started the conversation with this morning. Giving people labels and not seeing what the real connection was.

JC: Yeah.

BA: Was he politically oriented then? Was he aware of the 'politics?'

JC: No.

BA: So where would the 'Rightist' affiliation come from?

JC: His own convictions. And yet we never quarreled.

BA: How would the 'convictions of a Rightist' express themselves at the time?

JC: Just be against Labor.

BA: And yet he helped formulate the Guild. I wonder how he rationalized that in his own mind.

JC: He had a helluva definite idea of who was against him.

BA: Really?

JC: He was so violently against them that he fought against them tooth and nail.

BA: And 'them' in this case would be who: heads of studios?

JC: Anybody opposed to actors.

BA: So there really was this perception of the actor as something different?

JC: Oh, nobody knew what the hell they were.

BA: That's such a strange contradiction. That notion of being against Labor and yet picturing yourself as Labor. So there's Labor and there's Management, those are the distinctions?

JC: No. This was a personal thing to Bob. Management was Jack Warner and people that 'can't do that to me.'

BA: I see. Did you eventually get into social situations with Jack?

JC: No. He would never have stood it.

BA: Not even in the latter years?

JC: No. He had different compartments for people. There were the actors opposing him, therefore they were Communists.

Mrs. C: Starting the Guild? That period was really kind of exciting. In fact, Montgomery and Cagney when they'd go out to a meeting they would have a gun, a man with a gun. Those were exciting days.

BA: The notion of running for office. Were you put in that position, how did it come about?

JC: No. It was just a question of having been there early. And looking for names at the head of the list, you know.

BA: Was there a Guild President before you?

JC: Montgomery.

BA: Montgomery was the first? The tenure was for a year and then there would be another election annually.

JC: Yes, that's right.

BA: You had established yourself and were known as someone who was in favor of some rights for the actors. It was all pretty natural that it gravitated toward you for President at that point. I spoke with John McGuire and they just started negotiations yesterday. Here we are, fifty years later and it's still going on. How's the foot today? Swelling beginning to go down?

JC: I guess so, yeah.

BA: Oh, that's good.

Jim was an early member when the Screen Actors Guild was established and was elected to the Board of Directors in 1933. The Guild was formed on June 30, 1933 and the first meeting was July 12, 1933. Before SAG the actors were working very long hours and not compensated or was given overtime for Holidays or Sundays. They were required to pay for their own way to and from locations, no restrictions on weather-permitting calls - you worked regardless. No pay for wardrobe fitting and tests. In March 1933 the Producers forced actors under contract to take a pay cut of 50%, and only received 1-3/5 cents to the dollar taken at the box office.

Cagney was later elected President in 1942 and 1943.

BA: So there were things being reported back on you.

JC: The one that gave the stuff to Louella Parsons was Maskoff.

BA: His real name was Maskoff? So the reality is there was a group of people who out in Hollywood laid claim that it was theirs and they did everything they could to hold onto it.

JC: Yes. That's the reality of it.

BA: They happen to be Jewish.

JC: Yeah.

BA: It has nothing to do with *all* Jews on the planet. But these particular individuals who also might have been Greeks. They held on.

JC: Yes, of course. Speaking of Greeks. Skouras!

BA: Right! I have reason. Cause my Dad was also Greek, he owned a movie theatre for six months in Jersey City. The guy that put him under was Skouras. My father went bankrupt because Skouras would not give him the 'A' pictures to run. So there were Greeks too, I'm aware of that.

JC: Again. We threatened his hold on the Pictures. Can't do that to *him*!

BA: Did you know him?

JC: Yeah. Arrogant son-of-a-bitch.

BA: See that arrogance again.

JC: Yeah (*laughing*).

BA: I guess there was such massive amounts of money and the power of the films even in those days they obviously were beginning to see that.

JC: Thank God that's past (*laughter*). Louie Mayer was dying and they were talking about him. He said he'd give a million dollars to have one more hour to live. And he would.

BA: I'm sure. I was wondering if somebody said to him, "How about two million?" (*laughter*)

Ronald Reagan appeared in Boy Meets Girls 1938. He became the 40th President of the United States from 1981 to 1989. He died in 2004.

The Early Years

DEC 1 8 1943

Skouras Tours Nation In War Loan Behalf

LOS ANGELES—Charles P. Skouras, president of National Theatres and chairman of the industry's part in the Fourth War Loan, is on a tour of the nation in behalf of the loan drive. He planned to preside at regional group meetings of exhibitors in Washington, D. C., December 16; Chicago, December 20, and San Francisco, December 23.

Accompanying him on the organizational junket are members of his staff: Rick Ricketson, vice-chairman; B. V. Sturdivant, campaign director; S. H. Fabian, chairman of the theatre division of the War Activities Committee; Fred Stein and Andy Krappman, assistant campaign directors, and Seymour Peiser, publicity director.

Just prior to departing, Chairman Skouras met with treasury officials to discuss details. Attending the meeting, in addition to the above, were Ted Gamble, national director of the war finance division of the treasury department; Howard Mills, treasury western regional head; Robert H. Moulton, treasury Los Angeles bond chief, and Ed Schreiber, WAC publicity director.

As another organizational step preparatory to launching the campaign, Skouras appointed 44 prominent industry executives to spark the drive in their respective communities. Named to serve were:

For the Pacific coast—Louis B. Mayer, Jack L. Warner, Nicholas Schenck, Joseph M. Schenck, Y. Frank Freeman, Henry Ginsberg, Nate Blumberg, James Cagney, Rodney Pantages, Robert H. Poole and Kenneth Thomson; New York, Harry Katz, A. Montague, William F. Rodgers, Barney Balaban, Joseph Bernhard, Thomas J. Connors, Ned E. Depinet, Leonard H. Goldenson, Gradwell L. Sears, J. R. Vogel and Richard Walsh.

Skouras article from Jim's personal scrapbook

Eloise & Pat O'Brien, Phil Regan, Alice Faye, Jim

CHAPTER 21

Real Gangsters

Mrs. C: I remember once when we were all sitting in Chasen's. I guess when it first opened and there was a group of people sitting at another table and it turned out that they were gangsters. I was quite surprised.

BA: I asked her how the tough guys of the world responded to you once that image started going out there.

JC: They liked me.

BA: Was there a place they liked to hang out?

JC: The upper classes. You want to take someone to dinner, Chasen's.

BA: Were you there at the opening?

JC: Yes.

BA: Mrs. C. mentioned that Bugsy Siegel used to live up the road from you.

JC: Yeah. He had deadly eyes. And he would visit the set just to call on me. I didn't want him around at all.

Noel Madison in *Doorway to Hell,* 1930

BA: Siegel's lady friend was Virginia Hill or Virginia Pine?

JC: Hill. Virginia Pine was the girl George Raft dated for a time.

BA: Do you have trouble with these particular times of Hollywood. Were they distasteful to you?

JC: Oh no. Part of the times.

BA: You seem to be hesitant.

JC: Reluctant. Phil Reed always had a gangster fix. He liked them.

BA: The actor Phil Reed?

JC: Yeah. He was fixed on gangsters.

BA: There were a lot of guys that came out there and set up house in those days and visited the Lot.

JC: Yes. Some got jobs in pictures as extras.

BA: Mrs. C. mentioned one story while you were watching the rushes of some movie, and there was an extra in the background. Suddenly his face came on the screen and he said, "Now the cops back East will know where I am." (*laughter*)

JC: Yeah. "Inspector Coughlin" will know where I am.

BA: Where was he?

JC: He was out here scouting the woods. Then Wayne Walker came on the screen and nothing startling about it.

BA: Do you remember who the hood was on the screen?

JC: Oh sure. Bob Mattier. French. Oh, those hams, hoods live it up before the actors, you know. We wouldn't make a living if it weren't for them. There was an actor he had a good face. Cockeyed. What the hell was his name? Madison, Noel Madison.

BA: Did they tell you that?

JC: Oh no. That was their behavior.

BA: I see.

JC: But actually, we made pictures, headlines. Something would appear in the press.

MZ: Did he ever tell you the story about George Raft helping stop a hit on Jim?

BA: George Raft?

JC: He was an honest man.

BA: Upfront, huh?

George Raft in *Each Dawn I Die*, 1939

JC: Oh yes. He did a picture and I wasn't in it and he was invited by somebody to have a drink. He said, "All right. You're probably trying to poison me." I saw that in the rushes.

BA: Do you remember who that was?

JC: Just another of the small part players.

Mike Lally

BA: Raft was a good dancer too, wasn't he?

JC: Yeah. Ballroom dancing. He did all kinds.

BA: What was his association with gangsters?

JC: He worked for them in many of the nightclubs. They wanted to drop a lamp on my head, and he heard about it. Went right to the head man. He said, "This is a right guy." Stop the slate against the Guild.

BA: Against which Guild now?

JC: Screen Actors Guild. They had a slate to put up against what we had.

BA: So they actually tried to take over from the inside?

JC: Oh no. I do remember them working like hell talking to the guys that were on our side, the tough ones and they appointed them sort of their bodyguards.

BA: So when you say they were putting up a slate, they got a group of people together that they wanted to run for office.

JC: That's right.

BA: Actors, though?

JC: Yes, actors.

BA: To ensure their winning. They figured they would drop a light on you. So they were intent on winning.

JC: At any cost.

BA: Then there was actually more than one faction at the time. The studios who didn't want the Guild at all. Within the Guild, there were different people who were trying to set it up.

JC: Oh yeah. That's how it was then.

BA: So there would be Mike Lally and his wife (Pauline Wagner, actress). Mike was an extra in *Ceiling Zero*. He perfected some kind of relationship with Spike O'Donnell to prove his loyalty.

JC: Yeah. Loyalty to a mobster.

BA: He arranged to steal a machine gun from the prop room.

JC: The property department.

BA: He threw it over the fence and no one ever knew or found out.

Mrs. C: They all met at Chasen's. One man that I was very chummy with was told where to get good coffee in England. He was going over there and got kicked out. He had to go. I died because they said, "He is a Chicago gangster, a mobster that killed 25 people!" I guess that was true in those days.

BA: What was their reaction to Mr. C.?

Mrs. C: Got along beautifully.

George Raft appeared with Jim in Taxi! 1931 and Each Dawn I Die 1939. He died in 1980.

Noel Madison appeared with Jim in Sinners Holiday 1930, Doorway to Hell 1930 and "G"Men 1935. While filming Sinner's Holiday, Noel said, he learned the "gangster lingo" from Jim. He died in 1975.

Portrait of Willie in vaudeville

CHAPTER 22

New York Bound

BA: You came to New York specifically to become a dancer?

Mrs. C: I ran away from school. I had a married sister in Chicago, and I was visiting her and met this couple. He was an Englishman and they were doing a lousy act in Chicago, Milwaukee and other places. I think we got $7 one night (*laughs*). Through them, I got introduced to show business. But I don't want this about me. My sister knew about show business and showed me around. She took me into Chicago to Loew's Theater to see the acts and I came out of there, and this is true, I came out of there and went walking down the street with my sister very depressed. Because I wanted to be up there too. There was a woman, I'm sure she's dead now too, kind of a little dumpy woman, she ran up behind me and tapped me on the shoulder and said, "Are you a dancer?" Well, what I did I know. I did it at school and at home. I said, "Yes," and she said, "Did you see that two act, two girls?" And I said, "Yes," She said, "Do you want a job?" I said, "Yes," and she said, "Come with me." I went with her, we went back stage, rehearsed the thing and I went on the next day in Milwaukee. From then on, I was on stage.

BA: Wow!

Mrs. C: Isn't that funny?

BA: It's fascinating. So you wanted to do it from the beginning?

Mrs. C: Oh yes, I wanted to do it.

BA: Had you done some dancing at all?

Mrs. C: Only school stuff. I was always interested in it. I've got a picture of me (*laughing*) with some ballet shoes wrapped with a ribbon all the way up to here (*laughs*).

BA: Is that right?

Mrs. C: I was always in little school plays or something. And my, we were as far away from dancing, my folks, my mother certainly, Scots Presbyterian (*laughs*).

BA: Oh boy.

Mrs. C: My father, Lewis Vernon, bless his heart, wonderful character. He says, "That makes you happy?" I said, "Yes." He said, "Grab it, we don't get much. We're here and gone, right through."

BA: So he did know.

Mrs. C: Oh yeah.

BA: Did you literally run away from your school?

Mrs. C: Yes. I took my Spring tuition money (*laughs*) and I went to New York. But this isn't my story. Please.

In a Vaudeville act with Willie

BA: Well, it's *the* story. Let's think of it as The Story. I'm serious about that. You know, because you turn a light on here and turn a light on there. But the light is on all of us as we move.

Mrs. C: I know. But I've always shied away from that.

BA: How old were you when you took that Spring tuition money?

Mrs. C: I must have been 18, 19.

BA: But you knew you were going to do it.

Mrs. C: No, I didn't. It was just spur of the moment. I had to do something to get out.

BA: Was it a specific incident that encouraged you?

Mrs. C: No.

BA: But you had your eye on New York.

Mrs. C: Well, after I visited my sister in Chicago, I did, yeah.

BA: Do you remember your first recollections of seeing the city?

Mrs. C: I took a subway ride, got on it and rode clear up to the end to what was the Bronx or something.

BA: That's right.

Mrs. C: And clear down to Brooklyn and back again (*laughs*). Anyway, it was fascinating.

BA: You were an adventuress soul.

Mrs. C: Oh, I was determined that I wouldn't stay in a little town.

BA: What was the town?

Mrs. C: Crawfordville, Iowa. I don't want my relatives reading it. What I wanted to see were the bootblacks in front of the Astor Hotel in New York City.

BA: By golly.

Mrs. C: I can remember that, isn't that funny?

BA: And did you?

Mrs. C: I sure did. They were gone when I got there, though. Not the ones I read about. Now they're up on high chairs, you know. But now they don't have any. You have to go inside, and downstairs.

BA: So New York then, you took in your stride?

Young Jim in vaudeville

Mrs. C: Oh, I was dying to get there. Now I'm dying to get away from it before I go.

BA: What were your first feelings about California when you first went out there, did you like it initially?

Mrs. C: Oh yes.

BA: Right away.

Mrs. C: Yes, I did. Oh yes. I wasn't very smart in those days (*laughs*).

BA: What do you mean by smart?

Mrs. C: Well, here's what helped me. My older sister lived in Chicago and I got to go on the train and spend my vacations with her in the big city, it helped. She took me to the theater, so that did something to me too.

BA: It must have been your first experience in the theater because they probably wouldn't allow you to see anything.

Mrs. C: I'll never forget how beautiful the chorus boys were (*laughs*).

BA: Ah, That's great!

Mrs. C: I said, "Oh my, aren't they handsome men." I lived with my sister to save money, I mean, dormitory or whatever. Weekends I worked in a candy store. Ate half the profits.

BA: But you were working, always working.

Mrs. C: Yes, I had to have a little money.

BA: There is one thing that the both of you were just constantly doing from the time you were youngsters.

Mrs. C: You had to. Oh, you couldn't sit down and say, "somebody take care of me." No one would. I had a middle sister, the shyest, scared to death of everything. No one else was like that. She was so shy, and when Jimmy was in probably one of his first movies, she went to the theater and when he came on, she got up and left. She couldn't stand to go through it, I guess. I don't know what that would be.

BA: That's an interesting thing 'cause she wasn't doing it from the moral standpoint.

Mrs. C: Oh no. Never.

BA: So you're from Iowa?

Mrs. C: Born there, Scottish Presbyterian. I remember I went to a little school dance. Egads, it must have been grade school. A little partying, a little hopping around. And my mother (Alta Vernon) came. I wanted to die, I just wanted to kill myself I was so scared. I was jerked out of that.

BA: There was no dancing allowed of any kind then?

Mrs. C: Oh no. We could on Sundays. We could take a walk but couldn't play the piano.

BA: Is that right?

Mrs. C: Things like that.

BA: Boy oh boy.

Mrs. C: But we did.

BA: Did you sing?

Mrs. C: No, I can't sing a note. (*Sings*): "Jesus just wants me for a sunbeam..." (*laughter*)

BA: (*Continuing the song*). I remember that. But in the act you did later on you had to sing.

Mrs. C: We had to. Neither one of us could sing. It's a wonder they didn't throw tomatoes at us. (*laughter*) Jimmy could put over a song which he did later, I mean, no voice.

BA: Did you do comedy?

Mrs. C: You know what we did, we did every bodies act we ever remembered. We stole everything. (*laughter*)

BA: So you took the subway and you went from one end to the other and now you were in New York. Where were you living?

Mrs. C: It was a side street, 46th, and 7th or 8th.

BA: I use to live on 46th.

Mrs. C: Yeah?

BA: Was it close to the theater district?

Mrs. C: I guess so.

BA: Do you remember your first job?

Mrs. C: Well, we both got a job in the chorus.

BA: Was the *Pitter Patter* thing your first job?

Mrs. C: Yeah.

BA: Oh, it was. Do you remember auditioning for it?

Mrs. C: No, not really. We were just in a lineup, and I got hired.

The young couple at the train station

BA: Suddenly you had a job.

Mrs. C: Yes.

BA: They paid pretty good?

Mrs. C: I went out and bought a suite for $200 and was getting $60 a week. (*laughter*) $1 down, a $1 when they called me.

BA: (*laughing*) Right. So you were earning your keep from the very beginning and it didn't take long.

Mrs. C: No, it didn't.

BA: Then you just showed up one day, stood up on the stage and you got the job.

Mrs. C: Yeah.

BA: And you were now in show business.

Mrs. C: Yeah.

BA: Was it called 'show business' in those days?

Mrs. C: We were in 'the theater'. On the stage.

BA: But you were considered part of that profession.

Mrs. C: Oh yeah.

BA: So you must have been kind of excited about it.

Mrs. C: I was kind of chunky and curls (*laughs*). Oh boy.

BA: You were then in *Pitter Patter* and do you remember when you first spotted Jim?

Marriage License 1922

Marriage License

Mrs. C: Yeah. There was a boy that I liked, Jewish boy, was awfully nice, I still like him. Wonder where the hell he is. He asked me to go to a party one night and I said I would go if I could go with that red-haired boy there (*laughs*). Wasn't that cruel?

BA: And he was there, he was within earshot? He heard?

Mrs. C: No, he went to Jim and said, "A gal wants to go to the party with you." Jimmy said, "I haven't got the money." And I said, "I have!"

BA: That settled that (*laughing*).

Mrs. C: Yeah. I use to keep a little book, don't write this, a little book of the money that I'd given Jimmy. 'Cause I was working, getting what $60. That was a hell of a lot of money in those days.

BA: It sure was.

Mrs. C: Well anyway, I still have that book. Never thrown it away about the money I've loaned him.

BA: That's wonderful. Do you show it to him every once in a while?

Mrs. C: No. Oh, I've got to find that. Sad little book. Life.

BA: So you hit it off right away, did you?

Mrs. C: Well, I certainly did. (*laughing*).

BA: You did?

Mrs. C: He had another girl, Nellie. His mother liked her and Jim had been going around with her. Then I inveigled him some way. The girl, bless her heart wore, Jim's always had a funny thing about women's hats. I remember he threw one of mine out of a hotel window once (*laughter*). Anyway, one night he went out with her because of his mother, and she wore the wrong kind of a hat and that killed Jim.

BA: It would have killed me too (*laughter*).

Mrs. C: Anyway, it's funny now, but gee wasn't then. And he sent his brother, his kid brother, Bill Cagney to take me out because he had to go with this other gal. I was so furious, I broke a mirror and a few things and everything else (*laughs*). I had to go out with Bill, that I didn't care about at all. He did nothing but tell me how wonderful the Cagney's were. (*Bill laughs*) He was what 16 or 17. Anyway, that was the first and last time.

BA: Suddenly the two of you were together, going together? When did the first notion of working together hit you?

Mrs. C: Bread and butter, I guess.

BA: So that job with *Pitter Patter* stayed for a while.

Mrs. C: Oh, not too long.

BA: So the relationship lasted beyond that show?

Mrs. C: Oh God, yes. We had an agent, I guess you'd call it that, and we put an act together. As I told you, we copied everyone's jokes and things.

BA: Do you remember how that came about?

Mrs. C: I'm sure it was Jim's idea. Then we went to California because my family were out there. I thought we'd go to Chicago on our way back to New York. Where show biz was and I had a sister. She would go away to Iowa in the summer, being a teacher having summers off. So we'll live in her apartment and won't have to pay rent. We didn't have any money to speak of. We got into Chicago, we sat up all the way, we couldn't afford a sleeper. Then we got there and my sister had rented her apartment while she was in Iowa. We went to a hotel and it was $16 a week, which was a mountain to us, you know.

BA: Sure.

Mrs. C: Then we'd go around to agencies. They'd say that in those days they wanted photographs for advertising. We didn't have any and we didn't have the money to buy them, but we did take them. I think Jimmy got some money from a very dear friend in New York. He sent us money ("New York medicine"). It wasn't enough to get us both back, so Jimmy left me in Chicago because he had a chance at a job in New York. That was it, and he went ahead. What did I do? (*laughs*) I don't remember how I got along. It couldn't have been long that Jim sent money to return to New York.

BA: How did you go out to California for the intention of you and Jimmy working there?

Mrs. C: Movies, not me, Jimmy.

BA: So this was not long after *Pitter Patter*.

Mrs. C: Not too long after.

BA: So there was this definite move to California to attempt to get into the movies, early on?

Mrs. C: Well, we'd try anything.

BA: Right, I sense that. That it was a matter of trying, always trying.

Mrs. C: Oh yeah. Always trying. His mother said to come back and be a soda jerk or anything, and I wouldn't let him. I just begged him. I said, "Don't you do it. Don't ever do that, don't ever give it up."

BA: Did you take the train to California?

Mrs. C: Yes. We had a good friend from *Pitter Patter* that went with us.

BA: Did you have an agent at the time?

Mrs. C: No, Jim did. He could tell you his name (Crosby Gaige). He can remember Nathan Skadelsy in 2B. (*laughs*)

BA: It's a great name.

Mrs. C: I never forget it either. I wouldn't believe it.

BA: That's what I told him yesterday. I said, "You can't be making these names up. They're too great." (*laughs*)

Mrs. C: Well that was in the back of a car at Pennsylvania Station. We were going to Long Island for some reason. How we got the money, I don't know. We were going to visit somebody and this man in the car, was sitting up there, you can only see the back of his head in part. Jimmy said, "You see that man up there?" I said, "Yes." He said, "I sat next to him in 2B." I said, "I don't believe it. I dare you." You know, he went up and spoke to him and said, "I'm Jim Cagney." The guy said, "Huh, who?" He never heard of Jim Cagney (*laughs*).

BA: So was it Nathan?

Mrs. C: It was! Nathan Skadelsky. That's the kind of memory he has, from a thousand years ago. My God! Crazy. Well, he's done things like that many times.

BA: And you had differences in food preferences too in those days?

Mrs. C: Oh, did Marge tell you that?

BA: Yeah. She mentioned that.

Mrs. C: He loved, oh what was that Jewish fish? I had never tried it. Later I had some Gefilte fish and I liked it! (*laughter*) Anyway, we were kids, he'd go to one restaurant and I would go to another and meet later.

BA: That's how you'd go out to dinner?

Mrs. C: Would you know of two young kids who would do that?

BA: That's wonderful.

Mrs. C: Fantastic.

BA: Yeah and you'd meet later?

Mrs. C: Yes. We used to go to a restaurant on 8th Avenue.

BA: When did you finally tie the knot?

Mrs. C: September 28, 1922.

BA: Here on this coast?

Mrs. C: In New York. Went up to City Hall. Here we have us sitting there with a great big row of people waiting to be called. A big pregnant woman. (*much laughter*) Oh God. Can't write that.

BA: (*laughing*) That's a wonderful scene.

Mrs. C: Oh boy. It was. Then the Judge or whoever it was calling off the names, he would say, "Miss" then he would stumble over the name and say, "Anyone here live on Terrace Street?" (*laughter*) Oh God.

BA: It's real romantic, huh?

Mrs. C: Oh, romantic, God.

BA: Then after you were married, you went right back on to the boards?

Mrs. C: Oh, had to, if you wanted to live.

BA: Was that then you were doing Vernon & Nye?

Mrs. C: We tried.

BA: When you say that you would steal from whoever you could, do you remember any acts.

Mrs. C: I remember we were doing the act, God knows where, maybe Philadelphia and the orchestra always left for the dramatic show. No music and we came on, there wasn't any orchestra. Then they all came tearing in grabbing their instruments and of course you couldn't dance to it and we had to dance. It was the opening dance and I was trying it and finally I stomped my feet and walked off and Jim got down and did Russian and everything else. (*laughter*) The orchestra finally got it together. But those things happened all the time. Crazy things. Did he ever tell you about working with Charles Bickford?

BA: Charles Bickford?

Mrs. C: He dyed his hair red for the part.

BA: Bickford did?

Mrs. C: Oh yeah. Jimmy didn't need to in those days. Who was that little bum that wrote the Tramp story? He was everything, writer, producer. A little bit of a fella. He lived out there in Toluca Lake.

Jim Tully an American writer. He wrote Beggars of Life, which was made for a play on Broadway, Outside Looking In. It played at the 39th Street Theater and opened on September 7, 1925 till December 1925. It ran for 113 performances. Little Red played by James Cagney.

Oklahoma Red played by Charles Bickford.

Outside Looking In Playbill 1925

BA: You had a taste and it was a good taste, you enjoyed it. Were they good days?

Mrs. C: Oh, I thought they were terrible. I said to somebody I never knew that these people who are in vaudeville are so tough.

Outside Looking In, Jim Tully author and Charles Bickford

BA: Really.

Mrs. C: I thought they were just awful. They swore, and everything that I never heard. I've heard 'em all since (*laughter*).

BA: I'm sure. So they were coarse?

Mrs. C: Oh yes. I didn't like it. No, I really didn't.

BA: When did you finally stop performing?

Mrs. C: It was after the *Grand Street Follies of '28*. Jimmy got that part as Little Red in *Outside Looking In* off-Broadway. Then Jim went into the the Follies of '28.

BA: It was somewhat of a success.

Mrs. C: Oh yes, it was. And then he got *Women Go on Forever* with Mary Boland.

BA: Were your friends show business friends during that time?

Mrs. C: Very few. We didn't see them after the show. We made new friends on each show we went in. Then Jim went into the *Grand Street Follies of 1928*.

BA: Do you remember seeing your first movie as a child and being attracted to an actor?

Mrs. C: Yes. Charlie Chaplin.

BA: Yeah. Did you have any favorite dancers?

Mrs. C: Actors? No, I don't think I really did. I remember some gal by the name of Mable Normand.

BA: Oh sure. Yeah.

Mrs. C: Blonde. She got the size of a house later. Mary Miles Minter, do you remember that name?

BA: Yes, I do, as a matter of fact.

Mrs. C: She was trying to be another Mary Pickford. Fatty Arbuckle, remember that name?

BA: Yes.

Mable Normand was an American silent film actress, screenwriter, director and producer. Her name was linked to two scandals. Not a suspect in either crime. Died 1930.

Mary Miles Minter was an American actress. Appeared in 54 silent pictures. She also was involved in scandal with Director William Desmond Taylor. Died 1984.

Mary Pickford American actress, producer. Died 1979.

Fatty Arbuckle an American silent film actor, comedian, director, screenwriter. Aquitted after 3 trials for the rape and manslaughter of Virginia Rappe. Died 1933.

Mrs. C: Then mom (Alta Vernon 1856-1927) moved to California in the early 20's after my father (Lewis Vernon 1845-1921) passed on. My two other sisters were already out there. Mom died in California but they brought her back to Iowa.

BA: Did she meet your husband early on? Did they get along?

Mrs. C: Yeah. In those days if you said anything Jewish or you know about Catholic things, Oh God. So I was trying to think what I would say. You know what I told her? He's an atheist. (*laughter*) That's true.

BA: That's wonderful. (*laughter*)

Mrs. C: I don't think I knew what atheist meant at the time.

BA: She condoned that?

Mrs. C: Maybe she didn't know.

BA: No, but I'm just saying given the other possibilities (*laughing*).

Mrs. C: Thank God I gave you a laugh.

BA: That's wonderful. That's great.

Mrs. C: I was scared to death to say Catholic.

BA: I'll bet.

Mrs. C: Isn't it all stupid? You know it's so silly. Well, you don't know that then. I wouldn't care if he'd been a Muslim (*laughter*), couldn't stop me.

Salvation Army Brigadier Wallace Winchell, Bickford & Jim

BA: And, of course, as his life went on, his own perceptions of what he was changed, too.

Mrs. C: Oh yes. (*giggling*) That stiff Scotch training and a father six-foot something. Tall and bossing everybody around.

BA: That's exactly the point, they couldn't help it.

Mrs. C: They couldn't help it.

BA: And it's hard for us too.

Mrs. C: Realize that.

BA: & **Mrs. C:** (*in unison*) Yeah.

Mrs. C: I know Aunt Sadie lived out there, she's dead many years now, but in those days I was in the East and I went out there. In fact, I have a bedspread of hers that she made, beautiful. When was that earthquake: '33?

BA: Yes.

Mrs. C: Must have been around then because her little house jumped five feet off and she lived in the garage there for a while. But Aunt Sadie would never go to the movies. So I finally got her to go to one and I think Jimmy said "Damn" in it or something. Well she got up and walked off (*laughs*).

BA: Oh boy. You see, it's interesting what you just said, because you said Aunt Sadie would never go to the movies.

Mrs. C: Yeah. After I got a little money from Jimmy, later on I did a couple of things for her which she seemed to appreciate very much. She was a lonely old gal, my god. Uncle Isaac had died. A Scotchman.

BA: Did any of them ever pursue the theater?

Mrs. C: Oh, never.

BA: Not at all.

Mrs. C: No. I have one sister left. She's in a senior citizens home. She taught school and also taught swimming and horseback riding. When her husband died, he died at 52 and she had six kids, one son five girls. She got a job in a school that was one of those swanky ones, outside of Chicago. She would take a bunch of those ponies into Madison Square Garden for a show with some of the girls.

BA: You were always earning money?

Mrs. C: Oh, I had a little help. My father and mother.

BA: So your Dad, who was your support, was gone early on.

Mrs. C: Yes. Very. Jim worked always, soda jerking, anything.

BA: From the earliest days.

Mrs. C: Because of his father, you know about him?

BA: Yeah. I sense that talking about those early years, that so much of what he had to do, he did because he had to do it.

Mrs. C: Had to do it.

BA: And there was never any question?

Mrs. C: He told me before I really knew him, as a schoolboy he worked on Saturdays and Sundays in the New York Public Library. Those great big books weighed as much as he did. I often wonder if it had anything to do with his legs. But his were so strong in show business. Those books that he had to carry. Huge things weighed a ton.

BA: When people like yourself evolve, it's interesting because you were born in the midst of all that conditioning. And yet, you had the awareness to see beyond it.

Mrs. C: I wanted to get out. I had the nerve to do it.

BA: That's exactly the point. And that's what makes us keep moving in life, isn't it?

Mrs. C: I think so.

BA: Instead of getting stuck.

Mrs. C: Oh, definitely.

BA: So you saw this early on?

Mrs. C: Had it. Had it all. And didn't want it. I was born with something in me that was against it all.

BA: Or your ability to see beyond it.

Mrs. C: Maybe.

CHAPTER 23

Just A Job

BA: What we want to do is a film.

Mrs. C: On Jimmy's life?

BA: We want it to be Jimmy, as I write in those pages. Jimmy was an innovator. In truth, I liken him to a Picasso. He used a different kind of a canvas and he was an innovator just as much as Picasso was. They were both students of life. They watched life and they reproduced it as they could. The pages also say that if it's going to be a film about his life, it should be innovative.

Mrs. C: Yeah. I know.

BA: We want it to be unique to reflect the uniqueness of the man.

Mrs. C: That's nice.

BA: What we see in this is sort of a melding of a film and the stage. We want to take the theatricality of stage.

George Arliss in *The Millionaire,* **1930**

BA: We started talking about this yesterday with Mr. C. The transition that it must have been really different to go into the movie business as opposed to the stage business where there was no audience, there was a whole lot of fear, wasn't it?

Mrs. C: Yeah. But you know he was much calmer with the movies than he'd ever been on the stage. Entirely different person. It's a very funny thing. A live audience drove him into panic. As I told you, we had to keep a bucket there in the wings. He got so nervous.

BA: When he was a kid, obviously, attention was always on him and he liked to show off and you said he'd put on an act.

Lew Ayres in *Doorway to Hell*

Mrs. C: Yeah. Do Chaplin and things he told me.

BA: But on stage I guess the rush was a little too much for him and he would get apprehensive.

Mrs. C: Yeah. And yet even his first movie *Sinner's Holiday*, he was just as calm. But he didn't have anyone there but electricians and crew around and no audience. I mean, no real audience.

BA: Do you remember when the first feedback started to come in and you both realized that he had obviously connected in a rather grand way?

Mrs. C: It was after *The Public Enemy*. He first did a bit in *The Millionaire*. If it was three minutes it was long. He played an insurance salesman, a young man in a George Arliss movie.

With Edward Woods in *The Public Enemy*

BA: I remember seeing a picture cut from it. Arliss was a millionaire and he had a line in it, "If I were you, I know what I would do..."

Mrs. C: Well, get him to do Mrs. Arliss for you. Jim did her beautifully.

BA: How would the word come out? Doing a stage performance you would hear the applause and the reviews would come out that night and would know that you're a hit. In the movies it doesn't work that way, especially then.

Mrs. C: You'd go and see the preview and could sense it then. I think he just took a chance and said, "Well, this is a living, and I'll do the part." In fact, I later met Mrs. Arliss, she was a row ahead of us. I was with Jim. When he fell through the door there in *The Public Enemy* dead, Mrs. Arliss stood up and she said, "Jesus Christ!" In the theater, it shocked everybody (*laughter*). There was a murmur all over the theater. So you knew that it would make it.

George Arliss was regarded as Warner Bros. most distinguished actor of the era. He died in 1946.

With Jean Harlow

BA: You remember your first recollection of seeing him on the screen?

Mrs. C: Oh sure. Oh, I saw rushes and I saw previews.

BA: Would you discuss it with Jim?

Mrs. C: Not much. Just hope to God it was a hit. I knew it after seeing *The Public Enemy*. The author, Kubec Glasmon, Jimmy knows, they signed Louella Parsons' protégé Eddie Woods. Glasmon and Bright said, "No, don't want him." They saw Jimmy in *Doorway to Hell*, one of his first pictures, and said, "We want him." And they were the authors of the thing, they'd written it. They carried some weight, boy, so they put Eddie Woods in the secondary part and hired Jim. And that was that. *Public Enemy*. My God, then there was that gal, Jean Harlow. She was the big newcomer. She couldn't act for sour apples.

BA: Did you know her?

Mrs. C: Met her casually, that's all. Sat next to her in a nightclub, Roosevelt Hotel dining room. Chaplin was there too, but not with her. She had hair the color of this mat. She was never pretty, to me.

BA: You mean she was striking?

Mrs. C: Well, because she was a big girl.

BA: Really?

Mrs. C: Pretty big, yes. Or it seemed to me at the time. But she wasn't pretty like de Havilland. I never thought Rita Hayworth was very pretty.

BA: Really?

Mrs. C: No, but men did. That poor devil now has Alzheimers.

Rita Hayworth appeared with Jim in The Strawberry Blonde 1941. She died in 1987.

The Public Enemy with Donald Cook

BA: So the point that I mentioned to Mr. C. yesterday, is that you read all the books about the career and everything and how he saw it as just doing a job.

Mrs. C: Just a job.

BA: And getting to know you, I sense that same grounding was there with you, too. You saw it as what was going on.

The Strawberry Blonde with Rita Hayworth

Mrs. C: Yes.

BA: I kept looking for something else, you know, saying it can't be just that. And he'd say no, no, it was just that. I think that is the story. I think that is what is important today where we lay so much emphasis on fame.

Mrs. C: Yeah, you hit it.

BA: That's the way films should be.

Mrs. C: A job. Like waiting on a table in a restaurant.

BA: Exactly that. The structure of the film will be three major areas: the early years, the song and dance/vaudeville years - with yourself, and then, of course, the movie years. With a special emphasis on the formation of the Screen Actors Guild. I believe as you said, those were exciting times. There was a real-life excitement going on.

Mrs. C: There certainly was for me. It was for everybody then. Oh boy, that was kind of frightening, you know, 'cause we never had anything like that. Having a bodyguard sitting in your living room all night.

BA: Whose idea was that to have a bodyguard?

Mrs. C: It might have been Bob Montgomery. I wish Bob were alive, he could tell you. Oh God, he was wonderful. Oh, I liked him very much. He was never liked a lot by Californians. They thought he was a snob. He couldn't help it.

BA: No, that's who he was.

Mrs. C: But he got along with Jim, but they all said, "Jim how can you make a pal of a man like that, I don't understand it." Jim was very fond of him, same with Bob.

BA: As a matter of fact, didn't he have a home up here?

Mrs. C: Oh yes, right over here in Millbrook.

BA: Oh really?

Mrs. C: Ireland bought it. That Ireland who owns the big stores in Toledo. He bought the house. Lovely. Then they moved 30 miles from here to East Canaan, Connecticut. Buffie, his second wife lives there now. Skip his son, Robert Jr, he lives in Florida, he has a market.

BA: Really?

Mrs. C: (*laughs*) Yeah. He has a family too, married twice, I think. Buffie lives in this beautiful place and Bob's ashes are there. They had a ceremony, no preacher or anything. I think in the days from when he was in the Navy.

Mrs. C: A Commander spoke, just friends attended. We sat around in a circle and then a very young man who had known Bob up here talked. He said things about how they used to go hunting, you know, things like that, and no religion. He was one of those atheists (*joking*), I think it was. (*laughter*). His first wife Betty Allen, (Elizabeth Allen), was in show business and her sister married the owner of Cushman Cake. Remember the Cushman Bakeries?

Elizabeth Allen was married to Robert Montgomery from 1928-1950.

BA: Sure I do? Don't they have a daughter too, Elizabeth?

Mrs. C: Oh, I never see Liz, she's another Bob.

BA: Oh really?

Mrs. C: Did I help any?

BA: Sure did!

Mrs. C: Did I?

BA: You got the biggest laugh line of the last few weeks, that's for sure.

CHAPTER 24

Hollywood

BA: What are your remembrances of *Footlight Parade*?

Mrs. C: Well, it was one of his first dancing things that people remember, isn't that funny? But he had fans like that, you know. Then those little funny things that they didn't think would amount to anything, and it did. At Warner Bros. with Blondell, Loretta Young, and all those other gals, Rosemary and Priscilla Lane, were wonderful. He did his first western with Rosemary.

BA: What was it?

Mrs. C: *The Oklahoma Kid*. When they gave the land in Oklahoma and people ran to grab their piece.

BA: Is that what it was about? I never saw that.

Mrs. C: It was fun. In those days, it was great.

MZ: A telegram came from Martin:

Visiting Martin Sheen in *Kennedy*

"**Dear Mr. Cagney:** On behalf of the entire staff of Kennedy I wish to express our deep appreciation for the extraordinary honor you bestowed on us by your gracious presence on the set this afternoon. For all of us, it was a never to be forgotten occasion and for me, I am very deeply felt personal tribute (sic), I shall be forever grateful. Thank you and God Bless you." – Martin Sheen

Footlight Parade with dancing partner Ruby Keeler

MZ: Isn't that cute?

Mrs. C: Oh, that's lovely.

MZ: I'll read it to Jimmy, but he's resting.

BA: He was concerned it wouldn't get here.

MZ: It was kind of cute of Martin.

Mrs. C: He's a good actor. One of the best young ones coming up.

BA: Do you remember talking to your husband about him and the possibility of him playing Jim?

The Crowd Roars with Joan Blondell, 1932

Mrs. C: No, I didn't know who Martin Sheen was.

BA: What's your first recollection of him?

Mrs. C: Yes, I can tell you that. Remember an actress, Sylvia Sidney? Well, we were in Philadelphia and Jimmy was being honored by the American Diabetes Association with a Lifetime Achievement Award. It wasn't too long ago it was at the Franklin Plaza Hotel. So here's Jim, right in the middle of the thing and here's Sylvia Sidney and Martin Sheen sitting with us. Well, I tried that whole dinner to speak to Mr. Sheen and she wouldn't let me. She would grab his lapel to pull him around to say something, she was as mean as dirt. I thought, well honey, you're never going to hear from me ever again. I'll never pick you.

The Early Years

Taxi! with beautiful Loretta Young, 1932

In *The Roaring Twenties* with Priscilla Lane, 1939

Rosemary Lane in *The Oklahoma Kid,* 1939

BA: Were you friends before?

Mrs. C: No, never. I knew who she was, naturally, but I don't know if she was high or not, maybe she was. But that was my first introduction to Martin Sheen and I wasn't even introduced to him. No one introduced me. I couldn't introduce myself because I couldn't get him to turn around to look at me because of that gal. He was trying to be nice.

BA: For sure, knowing him.

Mrs. C: But she wouldn't have it. I guess Jimmy wouldn't talk to her, so she was going to get somebody, by God.

BA: So Cagney was on the other side of Sidney?

Mrs. C: Yeah. Sylvia Sidney.

Sylvia Sidney was in Blood on the Sun with Jim in 1945. She died in 1999.

Blood on the Sun with Sylvia Sidney, 1945

BA: Had they met yet? Had Mr. Cagney and Martin met yet?

Mrs. C: I think so. Jimmy picked him out and told me about him, but I didn't know who he was at the time. "There's a young fella coming up. There's something, he's going to make it." You know, one of those remarks and I knew it then when he said it.

Attending a Movie Premiere

BA: Well, in those early days, though, when you first went out there, it had to be different from New York?

Mrs. C: Then from how it is now, you mean? Different in what way?

The Early Years

With Bill Cagney, his Manager

BA: Well, we were talking about it this morning. The general change in people. They were a little more open in those days.

Mrs. C: Well, I don't remember him coming home and having any serious difficulty or anything with an actor, only with Warner Bros. He got along always with actors.

The Cagney's & The McHugh's

BA: Did you ever go visit him on the set when he was working?

Mrs. C: Oh yeah. Not too much. Paul Muni, I remember, he had his wife there all the time. I guess she coached him or something. When he did the Arliss bit that time, I was there. Sometimes I would go in for a few minutes and then, I hate that. The little wife looking to see what she could see, and all that stuff. It's crazy.

BA: What would bring you down there?

Mrs. C: Oh, mob scenes did mostly. I like things going on. I don't like just the two seats. Or a big crowd of some kind, that was fun.

BA: Do you remember one in particular that you observed?

Mrs. C: The picture he made with Raft. Newspaper picture with George Raft. That was a pretty good picture too.

The O'Brien's & The Cagney's at Santa Anita Race Track for the Opening, 1940. They had their own box and were stockholders.

BA: Were you friends with him too, Raft?

Mrs. C: Jim was. Raft did a very nice piece in the *Saturday Evening Post* in those years about Jim. It was very nice. Then somebody said, look out, they were going to drop a big light in the scene on Jim, would've killed him.

BA: Because of the Guild thing?

Allen Jenkins in *Mayor of Hell*

Mrs. C: No. I don't think it was the Guild. Ask Jim about that.

BA: Why did they warn him about somebody going to hit him with one of those enormous lights?

Mrs. C: Scare tactics, I guess. In those days they lit the sets, kind of what they use today. Raft lived down the street from us on Coldwater Canyon. Very nice house. His girlfriend was Virginia Pine.

BA: Bugsy Siegel's girl was Virginia Hill?

Mrs. C: Yeah. He rented a big house by the edge of Beverly Hills. He had his family with him and he had a young daughter. He would teach her how to ride a horse. A family man, really.

George Meeker

BA: Did you meet him?

Mrs. C: I didn't. Jimmy had.

BA: Who were your cronies or friends in those days?

Mrs. C: The McHugh's, the O'Brien's, Meeker's, George Meeker's. You wouldn't know him, he played small parts. Allen Jenkins and Mary.

George Meeker was in The Roaring Twenties and Yankee Doodle Dandy. He died in 1984.

Frank McHugh was in 11 movies with Jim, more than any other actor.

The Crowd Roars, 1932
Footlight Parade, 1933
Here Comes the Navy, 1934
Devil Dogs of the Air, 1935
The Irish in Us, 1935
A Midsummer's Night Dream, 1935

Boy Meets Girl, 1938
The Roaring Twenties, 1939
The Fighting 69th, 1940
City for Conquest, 1941
A Lion is in the Streets, 1953

Frank McHugh died in 1981.

Pat O'Brien and Jim did 9 movies together.
Here Comes the Navy, 1934
Devil Dogs of the Air, 1935
The Irish in Us, 1935
Ceiling Zero, 1935
Boy Meets Girl, 1938
Angels with Dirty Faces, 1938
The Fighting 69th, 1940
Torrid Zone, 1940

Ragtime, 1981

Pat O'Brien died in 1983.

Allen Jenkins was in 5 Cagney movies.
Hard to Handle, 1933
Mayor of Hell, 1933
Jimmy the Gent, 1934
The St. Louis Kid, 1934
The Irish in Us, 1934

He also appeared as a chorus boy in Pitter Patter, 1920. Allen Jenkins died in 1974

Frank, Pat & Jim

BA: So you have been buddies for a long time?

Mrs. C: Oh, the early 30's in California. Yeah. Pat O'Brien, Frank McHugh and Cagney, you know the 'Three Musketeers'.

Mr. & Mrs. Frank McHugh's home is made happy by Susan, Michael and Peter McHugh.

McHugh Family 1936

BA: Then you had your own group.

Mrs. C: Oh yes, me and Eloise O'Brien. When the men would get together, Eloise and I would be together. We were knitters and crocheters. I made God knows what all. I was always making, sewing, embroidering, crocheting, knitting. Dorothy McHugh was another.

BA: Did you hit it off right from the very beginning?

Mrs. C: I think we did. Dorothy has a son, he's a professor up in Toronto, the University there. Then she adopted a girl, Susie, and she works in New York. She's pretty clever with pen, with horses. Draws nothing but horses. She has a job there, a good, clever gal. Then she had Michael, who was Frank's. And that awful thing happened. God! The three women were like the three men, you know, together.

BA: Where was Eloise from?

Mrs. C: Iowa.

BA: Really?

Mrs. C: Around Des Moines.

Ralph Bellamy in *Picture Snatcher*, 1933

Mrs. C: I want to tell you about Dorothy McHugh, she's got a marvelous sense of humor. Here's an example of it. Now she always was crazy about Frank McHugh, her husband, and he had died. She's at the little village of Cos Cob, Connecticut, having to buy some groceries. She went by this man who waited on her for years, young rube, and he said, "Oh, good morning, Mrs. McHugh. I was so sorry to hear about your mishap." (*laughter*) She couldn't wait to get home so she could call me. "Mishap, isn't that wonderful!" God Almighty. She is just wonderful. Humor is just great, grand. It wasn't for Frank, she was just born that way.

At the AFI Tribute to Jim with sister Jeanne and A.C. Lyles, 1974

BA: They must have been quite a pair between the two of them.

Mrs. C: She was from up there in Hartford, Connecticut. She still owns the Hartford Turbine Works. She wanted to be with Frank in that little bitty house she's in now.

BA: So she stayed down there?

Mrs. C: Yes. Kept the house. Well, all her past is there.

BA: Does she live alone?

Mrs. C: Yeah. She has a son by a first husband who lives in Canada. He has children and, of course, Frank's son. The only McHugh child was killed at 21 years old in a car crash. We went through that. We had just gotten this house in 1955. Oh, that was awful. I didn't think they'd ever get over it. I don't think they ever did. Financially, she's a very wealthy woman. Her father invented all the big vacuum cleaners for hotels and all that kind of stuff. So that way, she's got it. We had very few very intimate friends. There were several people we might have dinner with, then we never saw them again. Bellamy (Ralph), when he came out here, we went through two wives with him. I guess he's had four. (*laughter*) Who else? Did you ever hear of the name A.C. Lyles? Do you know him?

Ralph Bellamy was in Picture Snatcher, 1933 and Boy Meets Girl, 1938 with Jim.

Ralph Bellamy died in 1991.

BA: I've met him.

Mrs. C: Well, he's an odd character.

BA: I've met him and his wife.

Mrs. C: Martha, yeah, I like her. A.C. just loves to grab onto somebody who has a name. He was in Alan Ladd's pocket for I don't know how long. And the poor guy dies at 52.

BA: Yeah, he was a young man.

Mrs. C: Liquor. That Susan, Susan Ladd, she's dead now too. That was the Ladd boys' mother. And David Ladd I think he's still around out there working. He worked his first picture at 12 years old. He worked with A.C. in one of those lousy little quickies, you know.

BA: Movies were still comparatively new.

Mrs. C: Talkies, yeah.

BA: Do you remember your response and reaction when Jim had made it big.

Mrs. C: Well, I just had such faith in the guy, that I just knew that this was it. After I saw the way *The Public Enemy* was received. He just seemed "made" for those parts at the time.

BA: Did life change at all?

Mrs. C: Not really. I don't think so.

BA: Certainly there was a public clamor for him and going out became problematic. He became more and more recognizable.

Mrs. C: Oh yes. When he came back to New York, the cabbies would say, "Hiya Red, Hiya Rusty!" They'd call him all those names. "Hiya Cag!" We went to the premier of *Yankee Doodle Dandy* and Mrs. Roosevelt was seated right in front of us. That was great!

BA: That must have been quite an evening.

Mrs. C: Yes, it was. It really was.

BA: What did Jim get for *Yankee Doodle*?

Mrs. C: I think it was $850,000.

Yankee Doodle Dandy, 1942

Mrs. C: I remember when we heard Constance Bennett was given a million dollars and we nearly fell over flat from that. Because she wasn't a big star.

BA: Boy, oh boy. Probably one of the first.

Mrs. C: I know Lombard was very popular and, of course, Gable, Gary Cooper and they still didn't get that kind of money.

BA: Well, I wonder who was the first to get it.

Mrs. C: Oh, I'll tell you, he's dead now. That Western actor. When I heard what he got, I nearly fainted.

BA: A Western actor? Wayne?

Mrs. C: Oh, no much later. John Wayne deserved it. He couldn't act very well, but he could ride a horse and his personality was terrific. It was William Holden.

William Holden was the first actor to earn one million dollars in salary and profit participation in 1957 for The Bridge on The River Kwai.

BA: But you personally used to shun the Hollywood parties and the Hollywood scene.

Mrs. C: Yep. I went and Jim went to a few. I can remember one party a big society gal, New York society, not a Vanderbilt or Whitney held. Maybe it was Barbara Hutton. Anyway, I hid behind a palm tree and listened to all the gossip (*laughs*).

BA: Do you remember what you heard?

Mrs. C: A few things, not much. Then that big girl who was the head of society there, Elsa Maxwell. We were at the party, John Barrymore was there with a young gal. I don't know whose house it was and on the landing was Ms. Maxwell. She had one of those recorder things taking everything down and she would ask actor after actress to come up and question them. And if they were high, or something, they must have said plenty. I remember John Barrymore was higher than a kite and that's a tragedy. Carole Lombard too, gosh. And who was that tall man . . . Jimmy did a picture with him, it was lousy? I hear he's a . . . what is that when a man dresses up in women's clothes?

Corinne Calvet, Dan Dailey in *What Price Glory?*, 1952

BA: A transvestite.

Mrs. C: Tall, good looking, blondish, in *What Price Glory?*

BA: Dan Dailey?

Mrs. C: Do you know he was that?

BA: As a matter of fact, I did know that.

Mrs. C: I was shocked to death. Lowell Sherman got very friendly with Jimmy. He said, "I taught Jim all about his hands." And I think Jimmy did copy his hands.

BA: I'm trying to think, Lowell Sherman was an actor.

Mrs. C: An actor. Big stage star before movies. Very good.

BA: So, Hollywood then was a lot different than it was now?

Lowell Sherman

Mrs. C: Oh my God. I don't even know Hollywood now. I don't know any of those young people.

Mrs. C: And they seem to make one picture and gone. It's entirely different. Very few that you see and see.

BA: What do you think there was then in the quality of the performer that's lacking now?

Mrs. C: Well, I think more earnestness and trying harder because they were trying to earn a living more than nowadays. A little gal, who's very pretty and cute and whatnot, can maybe do one picture and if she doesn't hit, why she's out. But another one can go on, if she gets good write-ups and all that business, then she's in. It's not like it used to be.

BA: Well, earnestness is a good word. People seemed more serious about their work.

Mrs. C: Maybe they were thinking about that next meal they had to eat.

BA: So there was something on the line.

CHAPTER 25

Awareness

BA: So you sense there's a difference between then and now? There's a difference now between the way people relate to each other?

JC: Oh sure. And I'm not the guy I was then either.

BA: You're not?

JC: No.

BA: What changes occurred in you? But you sense there's a difference in you now than there was then? A difference in attitude toward life?

JC: Yeah, oh yeah.

BA: Well one phrase that keeps coming up over the last few days, the way you seemed to be in those days was that you reacted to the moment. You were a man of the moment. You were functioning on the edge of things.

JC: I think so, yeah. Where, I don't know.

BA: Is there more caution now?

JC: Oh yeah.

BA: Yet there's still that element of the moment in you, I can sense that.

JC: Oh sure.

BA: I asked you the other day whether that element of the moment had anything to do with the way you acted. Your acting capacities.

JC: Oh sure. Grabbing anything and using it.

BA: Raw instinct almost. Just moving right at the edge. And it served you well.

JC: Had to.

BA: Do you think that real art is that? When art and life fuse?

JC: See the value of the moment.

BA: What do you think that requires to do that?

JC: To appreciate the full value as it happens.

BA: Alertness, awareness?

JC: Awareness.

BA: Which probably is a quality that in the city streets is developed for the sake of survival.

JC: I suppose.

BA: Then out here in the country, it's awakened for different reasons.

JC: It's all held in abeyance. (*Bill laughs*) What the hell are you laughing at?! (*Both laugh*)

BA: Speaking of awareness. I have a friend who talks about awareness a lot. The same man who I mentioned the other day who said, "Goodness appears to be out of fashion." To be good today is considered unfashionable. Did you ever come across a man called J. Krishnamurti? Does the name mean anything to you?

JC: Krishna yeah, the Indian.

BA: Well, he's a friend of mine and I saw him just a couple of weeks ago in Ojai. Did you ever meet him?

JC: No.

BA: Nice man. He says if you're good, people say you're out of step. Well, assuming awareness is the key, what's wrong now? Are we all deadened by this influx of technology and things so that we're just not awake? Was there less that we had to contend with?

JC: I think so.

BA: So would it be, it's out of fear that we're closing our doors?

JC: We're doing that automatically.

BA: We're in a defensive mode, more and more. Do you think we can stop it?

JC: Hard to say.

A tender moment with Bill

CHAPTER 26

Still Tough

MZ: D<small>ID YOU HEAR</small> what Dr. Brown told me this morning? For God's sake, I want to move this whole farm! Because he's so optimistic about you, and so am I. This sciatica, I told you, you see Jim from the times of flipping himself around and banging his body. He has all these spurs. I saw that in an X-ray they showed me in California. The spurs are all around the sciatic nerve. When that starts to act up, it used to hit the nerve and it would go down the leg and Jim couldn't walk. Now, from the thyroid, everything was going against him and it has come down into the foot. It's a pinched nerve that's doing this. It will get better. It does create a gout of sorts and he told me this morning that it's going to take a little time because of the circulation, but he's very optimistic about it. The pathologist told me the same thing yesterday, so it's great, it really is, don't you think so Jim?

JC: I guess so.

MZ: The first thing he told me yesterday is keep yourself busy mentally. So when the film gets going, Bill wants you to narrate part of it.

Lady

MZ: Lady (Lady was Jim's dog, a Shepard mix and was a very sweet dog) may only have an ear infection.

JC: Is that all she's got?

MZ: They think so, yeah.

JC: That's wonderful! Stop singing, everything goes blank.

MZ: You know what I just told my daughter? I said, "Karen, I had a feeling about Lady. I knew it wasn't a stroke because I took her blood pressure." She seemed so healthy that a stroke is going to have some symptoms before that. She has got ear problems. It could be the inner ear. It's like with Jamsie. A couple of months ago, he was always dizzy. Remember the dizziness, you don't have that now.

Lady, Jim's dog

BA: Probably fluid in the ear.

MZ: Yeah. But his, of course, was caused by the wrong medication.

White Heat, 1949

BA: You know when she was saying that you were flipping and jumping and you'd get the spurs. It came to mind the scene in White Heat when you're told that your Mom had died and you jump up and you start crashing across the table. Imagine how many spurs you got on that one scene. *(laughter)*

MZ: Can you stop for a minute. I want to tell you something. I'm on the phone with Tom Dunne. You know Tom Dunne is the fellow from St. Martin's Press and so I told him I'm calling him because I had a little talk with Doug Warren yesterday. I said, "I was going to try to use his book for your life story. But if it wasn't feasible, we couldn't do it." He said, "It isn't feasible, we don't have any money. We're a poor company and we're trying to get the book off the ground." Of course, every writer has his own direction. He said, "Marge that's marvelous." Then I said and also your publicity department called about doing the work. I said, "Publicizing the book, I never said we would", but I said, "Maybe." But I said, "If we do, on the condition coming from Mr. Cagney that Doug must be alongside of him." I said that because he should be. He wrote the book, he worked hard. They don't want him, they want you.

JC: I know that.

MZ: As long as he's beside you, it doesn't hurt, does it?

JC: No.

MZ: I said, "You'll have to fly him here, that's the only way we'll do it." And they agreed. He said, "You know what, Marge? A funny thing yesterday, I was taking a flight on American Airlines and the magazine we did an article for, of course, it was your Jimmy Cagney. They really blew it up and I was just curious so I walked by the people. Every time they grabbed the magazine to see who they were looking for, and they went right to your page. He said "There's such love for this man." Should I tell you that? I better not, you'll get a swelled head. But that's kinda nice, isn't it Jamsie?

JC: Yeah.

MZ: So the article and the response they got about your book, he said, "Was unbelievable!" Then he said, "Is it true you're doing a film on Jim's life?" I said, "That's right, it is true. That's why we were talking to Doug Warren. It's really happening. That Jim's very pleased and he says it's just wonderful." He said, "That everybody truly does love you." He said, "Of all the books that we had to promote, it was Jimmy Cagney's book that stood out front." Pretty nice, eh?

JC: Umm-hmm.

MZ: Oh, you're full of crap. Goodbye, I've got to go deliver some hay.

JC: Go do it.

MZ: I have to deliver some hay to somebody for their goats. Toodle-loo. I'll see you in a little while.

JC: Toodle-loo, kid!

BA: Then of course there's Marge. The ubiquitous Marge, ever protective of Jamsie and Willie. She told me, "Movie or no movie, Jamsie's health comes first, and in truth, it is the most serious and important consideration. But Jamsie is still Jamsie and he is determined to get well and make the movie. That's the way we make the movie.

CHAPTER 27

The Faraway Fella

The Story Behind the Picture
One day, out of the blue, Mr. Cagney suggested we take a little drive, he wanted to show me something. He guided us via a barely visible dirt road to a tiny one-room shack about a mile away from the main house.

This was his truly private hide-away studio he'd built himself out of old railroad ties, where he came to paint. You can see a bit of one of his works behind him. I recall feeling privileged for his having brought me there. This was, after all, a place that few, if any others had ever seen.

Then I spotted the statement beautifully carved out of wood: The Faraway Fella. He explained that was what he was called by his closest friend and acting colleague Pat O'Brien.

I'd brought my Polaroid camera with me (remember those?) and asked if I might take a picture of him with the sign. He said, "Sure!" It now adorns in this book.

The Far Away Fella

P.S. He also mentioned that the carving had been made and given to him by a friend and admirer, famous "malaprop" comic Norm Crosby, whom I also knew. So a few weeks later I sent Norm a copy of the picture. He loved it.

Epilogue

LIKE IN DREAMS, DREAM-LIKE *real-life events can also come to bizarre, irrational endings. This one began with a call to me a few days after I had returned to my home in Malibu and was back to working on the screenplay. I got a call, out of the blue, from a profoundly irate Marge. To put it in today's terminology: Marge was pissed. The cause? Apparently when I left Verney Farm at the end of my stay there, I left a piece of chicken in the refrigerator. That was it.*

At least, that's what provoked the semi-coherent tirade that followed which, as I recall, sounded something like:

Marge: "That piece of chicken is proof of what I've always known. You're incapable of writing the screenplay. . . or anything else, for that matter."

Huh?

Long…very long… period of silence. I had to say something.

"Sorry about the chicken," I replied, quite feebly, but honestly.

Marge: *"You should be!"*

> **Cagney & Sheen split**
>
> JAN 2 1984
>
> Fans waiting for the film bio of James Cagney are in for some bad news. The deal between Cagney and Martin Sheen, who was to portray Jim in a flick produced by Sheen's company, collapsed. Jim's associate, Marge Zimmermann, told the People Page that negotiations ended and the movie, based on Cagney's own book, "Cagney on Cagney" and the new book, "James Cagney—The Authorized Biography," may be taken up by another production company. Jim's life story is sensational. Cagney, now at his Dutchess County farm, just did a TV movie here, "Terrible Joe," about an old boxer. Jim loves our city streets. Born on the lower East Side, he was raised in Yorkville, *not* Hell's Kitchen, a mistake often made. He spent most of his life away from Manhattan, but always comes back to his old neighborhoods.

Another long period of silence. I suddenly remembered that Mister C. had a birthday coming up.

"Could I please wish Mister C. a Happy Birthday?" I requested.

Marge: *"Make it quick."*

A series of clicks...and then once again that always warm, inviting voice:

Cagney: *"Hey kid, I really miss our morning breakfast talks."*

"Me too, Mister C.," I said. "Just wanted to wish you a Happy Birthday. I'll be sending you a little gift to —"

The Early Years

Cagney: *(interrupting): "No need to send me anything except more of those wonderful pages you've been turning out. I'm particularly impressed with the transitions."*

Huh?

Should I follow what Marge said or what Cagney said? The answer to this seeming dilemma came crashing down that same day, with a phone call from Martin Sheen, who had just returned from attending a major shindig in New York honoring Cagney. Also in attendance were co-star Liza Minelli and co-producer Bill Greenblatt. Martin asked if he could come over, saying he had something important to tell me.

The "something important" had taken place the night of the shindig, during a limo ride back to the hotel which was shared by Martin, Liza, and Bill. Evidently, they had a contest during which each had taken a turn at dissing Marge and her strange ways. Liza won.

What Martin, Liz and Bill didn't know was that the limo driver worked for Marge. The following morning Marge pronounced the project officially dead.

The movie that began with such great expectations and promise about James Cagney's early years — that would have starred Cagney himself, never did get made, but thanks to Stone, Dayna and Lisa, the reader and I now have some wonderful memories of an amazing encounter I had many years ago with an amazing gentleman that we shall always have in this extraordinary book.

— *Bill Angelos*

Reflections from the Contributors

James Cagney has given me a great deal of joy since I was 12 years old. I will never forget tuning in to the AFI Tribute to him, eager to see what all the fuss was about considering that every major star in Hollywood was present at this event. After a few introductions and the wonderful montage of film clips, I realized that this was someone special. It didn't take me long to become captivated by his screen presence. I had no problem staying up all hours watching every movie and going to school feeling exhausted. It didn't matter, he was worth it! James Cagney's legacy is that he was so versatile. One minute he's gunning someone down, next he's singing and dancing across the screen. He did it all! Since then, I have become a serious Cagney enthusiast reading everything I can, and always hoping to find fresh information about him.

Well a few years ago, while surfing the internet, I stumbled upon an article written by a gentleman named Bill Angelos who described six weeks he spent with Cagney at his farm in Stanfordville, NY. *What?* I was floored! Why didn't I ever hear about this? I then messaged Bill and told him what a huge Cagney fan I was and he told me about this manuscript. After much communication, Bill allowed me to read it and said to share it and so I did with my fellow Cagney devotee, Dayna DeCarlo. We both had the same reaction afterwards: it was amazing! Bill asked us what we should do with it and we immediately told him he must publish it. Our mutual friend and writer Stone Wallace provided us with a great connection and got the ball rolling. The rest is history.

Reading this manuscript and participating in this project about James Cagney has been the thrill of a lifetime for me. I hope this work will encourage others to explore the world of James Cagney and discover what a great actor and human being he was. Thanks to my family for putting up with my daily Cagney fixes and special thanks to Dayna and Stone for all their work. And lastly thanks to Bill for sharing his wonderful experience with us.

– Lisa Sanita

Having been asked to do something of this size and magnitude was shocking and surprising to me. I confess I don't have any credentials in the field of writing, but I do know the subject quite well.

When Lisa found Mr. Angelos' article and we chatted with him, I was given the opportunity to read this wonderful manuscript. I felt very privileged and honored to have a once in a lifetime chance to read the revealing work he did with Mr. Cagney. I couldn't put the pages down, so many funny and never before things he revealed about the man through their many discussions. Mr. Cagney never ceases to amaze me.

The Early Years

I spoke to Mr. Angelos after finishing the manuscript and told him how wonderful it was. He said, "What should I do with it?" Lisa and I both said, "Publish it!" I thought this intimate insight into James Cagney's early life, his personal recollections, along with those of his wife, should be shared with other Cagney fans as well. He then said, "You and Lisa go ahead and get it published, I trust you both implicitly."

I never had such an interesting experience learning so much about book editing and all that went into extreme research. To work on a project of someone I've been a fan of since I was 12 years old (43 years in total) and having met the legend at his upstate New York farm was such a gift. Yet to my surprise it came pretty easily. So, Thank You Mr. Angelos for having such confidence in me and in making this happen. Thanks to Lisa Sanita, my partner in crime, and to Stone Wallace for your expertise and guidance. The wonderful SATC photos from Columbia University Archives researched by Jay Dubner. To my parents, Lois and Daniel DeCarlo for allowing me to stay up all hours of the night to watch classic James Cagney movies (as long as I went to school the next day).

And most of all to the greatest actor ever and an even greater human being. Thank You Jim!

– Dayna DeCarlo

James Cagney exploded into my life back in the fall of 1972 when CBC television began broadcasting as part of its late-night movie package a series called "Vintage Cagney". Up to that point I hadn't seen many Cagney films since our local stations rarely showed classic movies. The only two I could recall seeing were *Man of a Thousand*

Faces and *Captains of the Clouds*. Fine films and Cagney was good, but truth be told he hadn't made the same impression on me as had his old Warner Bros. co-star Humphrey Bogart, some of whose early films I *had* managed to see, particularly enjoying Bogie's gangster pictures. But when "Vintage Cagney" began airing at 11:30 pm on Monday night, I discovered an entirely new experience and found a new movie hero. The CBC catalogue primarily featured those Warner Bros. films Jimmy made between 1938 and 1942 (which I still consider his best period of filmmaking). There were comedies (*The Bride Came C.O.D.*), drama (*City for Conquest*), romance (*The Strawberry Blonde*), war (*The Fighting 69th*), crime (*Angels with Dirty Faces, The Roaring Twenties*) and even a rare Western (*The Oklahoma Kid*). The series ended just before Christmas of that year, with *The Public Enemy* being the final offering. During that two-month period I could barely get through the week, eagerly awaiting each new James Cagney adventure. And no matter what the genre, those movies never once disappointed me – nor did Cagney. While I still loved Bogart, Jimmy had become my Number 1 man. Of course the bonus was seeing these two favorites together in their three film outings, with poor Bogie usually on the receiving end of a Cagney bullet. Naturally I was disappointed when the series ended, but as far as James Cagney was concerned, I was hooked. Still am. All these many years later I am as hepped on James Cagney as I was as a 15-year old boy. Though I never personally met the man, the impact he has had on my life is enormous. Not just as a dynamic actor who influenced my own theatrical leanings, but for the truly good and decent person he was offscreen. He became my ideal of what a real man is. I wanted to share his values. Tough, sure. But he was also caring and compassionate, concerned about the world and its people. A dedicated environmentalist. A loving husband who enjoyed one of Tinseltown's most enduring marriages with nary a scandal attached to his name. Jimmy was a movie star in the truest sense of the word but remained modest about his success, claiming that it was just a job, a way to put the groceries on the table. Can't get much better than that.

I confess with no apology that I envy Bill Angelos for having had this incredible opportunity to spend time with Jimmy and speak with him about his early years, the years of struggle and finally achieving success, in the process uncovering many facts not revealed in previous books written about and by James Cagney. An extra bonus is Bill's talk with Jimmy's beloved wife Willie, who for the first time shared her recollections of her own life and those early years with Jim. What a gift Bill has given us by allowing these conversations to be published and made available to Cagney fans worldwide. And what a privilege it has been for me personally to pay my own tribute to James Cagney by assisting in this project with three great friends.

Thank you, Bill. Thank you, Dayna. Thank you, Lisa.

– Stone Wallace

Acknowledgements

Choosing photos for this project was extremely fun and rewarding. Searching for rare pictures of Jim during his early years (vaudeville, with his friends and wife) proved daunting at times, but well worth the effort.

I would like to thank all those wonderful photographers who throughout Jim's life span provided us with rare candid and touching photos of this great man.

Apeda Studio

Bill Angelos

Blackwell Island Archives

Columbia University Archives

Dayna DeCarlo

Hy Rubin

Bert Longworth

Mandy-Rascal

New York City Municipal Archives

New York Public Library

Paramount Pictures

Saturday Evening Post

Screen Actors Guild

The James Cagney Estate

United Press International - New York, Los Angeles, Boston

Variety

Warner Brothers Studio

Warner Brothers Studio Photographers

Wikipedia

20th Century Fox Studio

www.ingramcontent.com/pod-product-compliance
Lightning Source LLC
Chambersburg PA
CBHW071702160426
43195CB00012B/1554